SIMPLY VEGAN

D1638174

SIMPLY VEGAN

Authentic Vegan Dishes From Around the World

David Scott

Foreword by Carla Lane

Thorsons
An Imprint of HarperCollins*Publishers*

Thorsons
An Imprint of HarperCollins*Publishers*
77–85 Fulham Palace Road,
Hammersmith, London W6 8JB

Published by Thorsons 1992
10 9 8 7 6 5 4 3 2 1

© David Scott 1992

Illustrations © Lynne Farmer 1992

David Scott asserts the moral right to
be identified as the author of this work

A catalogue record for this book
is available from the British Library

ISBN 0 7225 2719 5

Typeset by Harper Phototypesetters Limited,
Northampton, England
Printed in Great Britain by
HarperCollinsManufacturing Glasgow

All rights reserved. No part of this publication may be
reproduced, stored in a retrieval system, or transmitted,
in any form or by any means, electronic, mechanical,
photocopying, recording or otherwise, without the prior
permission of the publishers.

CONTENTS

ACKNOWLEDGEMENTS

I would like to thank Eve Bletcher, creative chef, food researcher and stylist for her expert help in the preparation of this book.

Thank you to Carla Lane who, with her mother Mrs Barrack, is a regular customer at the Everyman Bistro, for her generous agreement to my request to write the Foreword to Simply Vegan.

Finally thanks to Jane Middleton and Sarah Sutton, the original and present editors of this book, for their support and enthusiasm.

FOREWORD
BY CARLA LANE

I particularly welcome this book because graduating from vegetarianism to being a vegan was hard for me.

David has put together something quite original, in that the recipes are not simply manmade but carefully selected dishes used throughout history in countries all over the world by nations who are natural vegans.

In the days of Man's relentless destruction of our planet and of the creatures who occupy it, it is important to encourage non-meat eaters – not only for health reasons but for the psychological well-being which eventually comes with the knowledge that they are not part of the cruelty involved.

This is a well-thought-out book aimed at making veganism easier; the faint-hearted will draw a new courage from its interesting recipes and the already converted will discover that there is more to a vegan's life than rice!

INTRODUCTION

The vegan diet, which excludes all animal and dairy foods, has quite a long tradition in Britain but its advocates have always been in a very small minority. In the last ten years, however, public awareness and concern about cruelty in animal farming and the health risks to humans from eating some animal products has grown rapidly, and there has been a parallel increase in the number of vegans and those sympathetic to their concerns. Developments in vegan cuisine have perhaps not kept abreast of this widening interest, and to many people who may otherwise be attracted by the idea, veganism is still associated with somewhat boring, heavy and tasteless food, relying on ingredients that can be obtained only from health-food shops. The intention of this book is to demonstrate to as varied an audience as possible that vegan cooking can be as flexible and delicious as any other style of cuisine, and that a wide range of vegan dishes may be simply prepared with ingredients that, with one or two easily available exceptions, would be found in an ordinary well-stocked kitchen. Recipes ranging from snacks to starters, to light lunches, main meals and dinner party dishes, are given here, as well as information on ingredients and basic cooking methods. The vast majority of the recipes are not adapted from other recipes containing animal or dairy products; they are vegan in their original and intended conception. Many are collected from foreign cuisines such as those of Southeast Asia, the Middle East and India, where for economic, climatic or religious reasons a lot of dishes are animal-product free.

This book sets out to provide a collection of interesting, varied, nutritious and delicious recipes not only for committed vegans but also for anyone else who, for philosophical or dietary reasons, wishes to prepare vegan meals either regularly or on an occasional basis. Perhaps such an introduction to the pleasures of vegan eating will lead some readers to more interest in the subject. If so, I recommend that they contact the Vegan Society at 7 Battle Road, St Leonards on Sea, East Sussex, TN37 7AA.

THE VEGAN DIET

Why Vegan?

There are three main reasons why people become vegans or wish to include more vegan dishes in their diet. Firstly, vegans do not contribute to the suffering of animals reared for their flesh, eggs or milk. Secondly, because animal farming is an inefficient way of using our natural resources many of the world's food shortages could be alleviated if land devoted to animal farming was turned over to plant cultivation. Thirdly, there may be health benefits from a vegan diet. This is particularly the case for sufferers from common food allergies, many of which are caused by foods excluded from the vegan diet such as dairy and meat products and the additives found in refined and packaged foods. Vegans eat only primary foods and thus they avoid the residues of poor-quality feed and chemicals sometimes given to animals (which if eaten by humans become foods secondary in the food chain).

Vegans and Nutrition

The vegan diet can successfully provide all the protein, carbohydrate, vitamins, minerals, fat and fibre the body needs to function at an optimal level. A mixed diet of whole grains and flours, pulses (and soya bean products), vegetables (raw in salads or lightly cooked) nuts, seeds and fresh fruit provides wholesome nutrients not denatured by overcooking or processing and uncontaminated by the added saturated fats and sugars found in refined foods. It should be emphasized, however, that to get the best out of a vegan diet you must make sure it contains a wide variety of different foods, of which a large proportion should be fresh or unrefined. A short resumé of the main nutritional groups with reference to the vegan diet follows.

The basic food groups in the vegan diet provide good complementary protein combinations, and a mixed vegan diet will contain enough high-quality protein for most human requirements. To ensure a good balance the source of the protein should be about sixty per cent grains, thirty-five per cent pulses and/or nuts and seeds and five per cent leafy green vegetables. These figures do not include nutrient requirements other than protein and for these the diet must also include vegetables (especially in salads) and fruit.

The intake of fats of any kind should be moderate and should consist mainly of vegetable oils such as corn, olive, peanut, safflower, sesame, sunflower and walnut. Cold-pressed oils and margarines contain more natural nutrients than heat-extracted oils. Finally, the best way to eat fats is in the state in which they occur naturally, i.e. as part of the structure of nuts, seeds, whole grains and beans.

Carbohydrates are the body's main source of energy. Such foods as wholegrain cereals and flour products (wholemeal bread, wholemeal pasta, etc.), pulses, vegetables (especially root vegetables) and fruit are good carbohydrate sources. A proper mixed vegan diet will supply all the necessary carbohydrates, and it won't leave that craving for more that is often the result of eating refined foods.

A balanced vegan diet of fresh and whole foods will provide all the vitamins and minerals the body needs with the possible exception of vitamin B12 and calcium. Vitamin B12 differs from other B vitamins in that ordinarily it is found naturally only in animal products. There is in fact no evidence that vegans suffer from B12 deficiency any more than other groups, but the body can store several years' supply of B12 so long-term research would be needed to discover the B12 needs of people new to the vegan diet. To be on the safe side, non-animal sources of vitamin B12 are miso (fermented soya bean paste), brewer's yeast (available in tablet form), sea kelp, some commercially available vegan foods such as Barmene and Tastex (both yeast extracts) and soya milk (e.g. Plamil), and cask-conditioned draught beer. It is also possible that over a number of years vegans begin to produce their own B12.

There is no evidence to show that vegans as a group suffer calcium deficiency, but because the diet excludes milk and cheese, two common sources of calcium, some people worry about their calcium intake. Rich natural sources of the mineral are buckwheat, wheatgerm, brewer's yeast, watercress, fennel, leeks, spinach, almonds, brazil nuts and figs.

Many other foods contain smaller amounts of calcium. Finally, one of the best ways of maximizing the body's absorption of calcium is to take regular exercise.

Children and the Vegan Diet

Many vegan parents have brought up healthy and happy children on a vegan diet, but it is important to be particularly careful to ensure that babies and very young children obtain all the nutrients they need. Parents who have recently become vegans would be unwise to change the diet of very young children suddenly to a vegan one without the supervision of a nutritional expert. Those with experience of the vegan diet will need only to take the sensible dietary precautions required of anyone bringing up children.

Main Vegan Foods

- Grains and grain products such as bread and pasta.
- Pulses, a group which includes all the varieties of beans, peas and lentils and their products such as soya flour, soya milk, bean curd and soya sauce.
- Vegetables, cooked and raw, and vegetable oils and margarines.
- Sea vegetables and their products, such as agar-agar.
- Nuts and seeds, nut and seed spreads such as peanut butter and tahini, nut and seed oils and margarines and nut milks.
- Fruit, both fresh and dried.
- Mushrooms.
- Herbs and spices.
- Vinegars, sugars, syrups, mustards, pickles and chutneys.

Note Honey is produced by bees and as such could be classified as an animal food. However, some vegans dispute that taking honey from a hive and replacing it with sugar and water is cruel to the bees. Furthermore, bees are not killed in the process and they lead a natural life. The arguments for and against have resulted in disagreements and some vegans use honey, others do not.

UNUSUAL INGREDIENTS AND TECHNIQUES

The vast majority of recipes in this book require no special ingredients but a few do use items with which people new to vegan cooking may be unfamiliar, or they may use vegan substitutes for dairy products. Such ingredients are listed here, together with information on a few simple techniques.

Beansprouts

When beans or other seeds such as alfalfa are sprouted their nutritional value increases. During the sprouting process the dormant seed germinates and starts to grow and the B complex and vitamin C content increases, amino acids are produced, fats are converted into water-soluble compounds and enzyme activity increases. Fresh beansprouts thus contain many of the nutrients lost from other foods during cooking and they make a healthy addition to a diet otherwise based on cooked or processed meals. (Francis Chichester supplemented his diet with beansprouts during his round-the-world boat trip aboard *Gypsy Moth*. He designed a special compartment in the galley for sprouting.) The other great advantages of beansprouts are that they are quick, simple and cheap to grow and available all year round. Mung beansprouts are the most commercially popular variety and the beansprouts we are most familiar with in Chinese restaurant dishes. Other non-commercial favourites are chickpeas, kidney beans, soya beans and lentils. Mixtures of beans may also be sprouted to add variety to the taste and texture of beansprout dishes. Aduki beans, lentils, chickpeas and mung beans is a popular mix. Whole grains such as rice, wheat and oats can also be sprouted but they should be briefly cooked by stir-frying or steaming before eating. Fenugreek, alfalfa, sunflower and sesame seeds all sprout well and are delicious fresh or gently cooked.

Serve beansprouts fresh in salads or sandwiches and cooked in stir-fry dishes. They are also good in soups and casseroles, wrapped in thin pastry sheets as in spring rolls, or gently chopped in a food processor and added to bread dough before baking.

To sprout beans, grains or seeds (general method)

Place beans, grains or seeds (for amounts see below) in the bottom of a large, wide jar and half-fill it with water. The sprouts will be 6 times as bulky as the unsprouted beans, so make sure the jar is large enough. 1 oz (25g) beans will make approximately 8 oz (225g) beansprouts. Leave them to soak overnight and then drain the water away. Rinse the beans and drain again. A piece of cheesecloth placed over the mouth of the jar and secured with an elastic band makes this job easy. Now place the jar in a warm, dark place (about 70°F (20°C). Repeat the rinse and drain procedure 3 times a day for 3 to 5 days. The length of time before the sprouts are ready depends on the bean used and the stage at which you decide to harvest them. After this time mung beansprouts will be about 2 in (5cm) long, while sprouts from chickpeas, lentils, kidney beans and soya beans will be ½ in (1.25cm) long. Spread the beansprouts (drained) on a tray in the daylight (indoors) for 2 to 3 hours. They can now be used as required. Store unused beansprouts in a covered container in the refrigerator and rinse before serving. They can be used fresh for up to 3 days or cooked for up to 5 days after harvesting. If you have 2 jars available for bean sprouting you will have a constant source of fresh beansprouts available. Scald used cloths and jars before re-using to avoid spoiling the next batch.

Suggestions for Sprouting

Pulses	Grains	Seeds
Aduki beans	Barley	Alfalfa
Broad beans	Corn	Fenugreek
Chickpeas	Millet	Sesame
Haricot beans	Oats	Sunflower
Kidney beans	Rice	
Lentils	Rye	
Mung beans	Wheat	

Approximate amounts to use in each batch:
Pulses — 2–3 oz (75–100g)
Grains — 3 tablespoons

Seeds — alfalfa, 1 tablespoon; fenugreek, 3 tablespoons; sesame, 3 tablespoons; sunflower, 6 tablespoons.

Binding Agent

Where a binding agent is needed and egg would conventionally be used the vegan substitute per egg is a mixture of 1 tablespoon soya flour and 1 tablespoon arrowroot creamed in a little water.

Coconut Milk

Coconut milk, an ingredient in some Southeast Asian and Indian recipes, is not the liquid inside a coconut, which is called coconut water, but is rather the liquid pressed from grated coconut flesh and diluted with water, or obtained from dried coconut after it has been soaked in hot water, milk, or a mixture of both. Tinned coconut milk is generally available from Chinese or Indian grocery stores. Use the unsweetened variety. Stir it before use. The quality is as good as that of coconut milk made from dried coconut or from the so-called 'fresh' coconuts available in the UK. A reasonable substitute for coconut milk can be made by blending creamed coconut with water, 4 oz (100g) creamed coconut to 12 fl oz (350ml) hot water.

Margarines and Vegetable Oils

For vegan cooking, choose vegetable margarines that do not contain whey or caseinates, both of which are dairy products. Vitaseig, Granose and Suma margarines are suitable for vegan use. Vegan shortening and suet, such as Nutter and Suenut, are available in health-food stores.

For the recipes in this book I recommend that you use additive-free, unhydrogenated and, if available, cold-pressed vegetable oils such as sunflower, sesame, safflower, and the more strongly flavoured olive oil. These partially unsaturated oils supply essential fatty acids and there is some evidence that they reduce the build-up of cholesterol. Because they are not artificially hydrogenated or treated with antioxidants they will go rancid more quickly. Store in the refrigerator and do not buy too much at one time.

Nuts

Nuts are the fruits or seeds of certain trees or bushes. They normally consist of just a hard or tough outer shell enclosing an edible kernel –

the nut – but some, such as the almond or walnut, correspond to the stone of, say, a peach or plum, and are surrounded by a fleshy layer while on the tree. Others such as the pine are born 'uncovered' (in the cones of pine trees), while the Brazil nut, which has never been successfully cultivated commercially, is found by the dozen in a pod so heavy that collectors in the Brazilian forests protect themselves from falls with helmets and shields.

Collectively nuts have a nutritional value similar to cereal grains in respect of their high vitamin B complex, fibre and protein content. The protein, however, as in cereals, is deficient in lysine and is thus most effectively used if the nuts are eaten with a complementary food source such as pulses. In fact, most nuts are high in fat and this together with their relative scarcity rules them out as a main protein source. Hence their primary use as garnishes, flavourings and snacks. Exceptions to this rule are chestnuts and acorns, both of which are low in fat and high in carbohydrate. Ground into flour, they can be used to add flavour to grain flours or as ingredients in their own right. The Arabs also use ground nuts to thicken savoury or sweet dishes but they have traditionally used the more expensive and exotic pistachio or almond.

Nuts keep better when bought whole and unroasted. Their high fat content makes them vulnerable to rancidity and although freshly ground nuts have the most flavour, exposure to air quickly leads to loss of taste. Thus grind nuts yourself as and when needed or buy ground or crushed nuts vacuum packed and use quite soon after opening. The cheapest way to buy whole nuts is loose from a shop that sells them in bulk. Broken nuts, which are perfectly good for most cooking purposes, are often cheaper than the whole variety. Store nuts, whether cooked or raw, in glass or plastic containers in a dark, dry and cool area.

Most nuts, apart from walnuts, taste much better when lightly roasted or dry-fried. They are also easier to grind or crush after roasting.

Dry-roasting nuts

To oven-roast, preheat the oven to 375°F (190°C, gas mark 5). Spread the nuts on an ungreased baking sheet and place them in the oven. Roast them for about 5 minutes or until lightly browned. Shake the nuts around once or twice during this time.

To pan-roast, put the nuts in an ungreased heavy frying pan and gently toss them over a moderate flame until lightly browned all over.

Grinding and chopping nuts

Grinding nuts is most easily done with an electric grinder or blender but a manual grain grinder is fine. For coarsely grated nuts put a small amount at a time into an electric grinder or blender and switch the machine on for a few seconds only. For more finely ground nuts leave the machine on for longer. Alternatively, for small quantities use a pestle and mortar or wrap the nuts in a clean cloth and roll them with a rolling pin.

To slice nuts, cut them individually with a sharp knife. If they are very hard, soften them by boiling them for a minute or two.

The best way to use and enjoy nuts is to experiment with small amounts of different varieties in your favourite salads, casseroles, grains and gratin dishes. Try them in fruit salads, crushed in sandwiches, as thickening and flavouring agents in soups and stews, or mixed with dried fruits as a snack.

Sea Vegetables

Seaweeds are better named sea vegetables since weeds tend to be unwanted plants. Sea vegetables absorb and concentrate nutrients present in the sea and they provide a plentiful supply of vitamins A, C, D, E and K, plus B complex vitamins, including B12 – vitamins rarely present in land vegetables. They are rich in minerals, including potassium, iron, magnesium, copper, zinc, calcium and manganese. In Japan sea vegetables are valued as antidotes to the effects of radiation exposure and for the protection they can give the body from the effects of toxic substances. Sea vegetables are also exceptionally alkalizing and useful for combating acidity caused by overconsumption of coffee and alcohol.

In Japan, sea vegetables as foodstuffs are commonplace and their use is taken for granted. In fact *kombu* is packaged in fancy boxes and may be given by appreciative guests when they go to a friend's house for dinner. Japan has developed the culinary potential of sea vegetables more than any other country and their coastal waters are successfully farmed for all the common sea vegetables. As a result, the Japanese dominate the sea vegetable market and they are the major source of supply to our own health-food shops and other stockists. For this reason the details given here will refer by their Japanese names to the sea vegetable species discussed, e.g. *nori, wakame, hijiki* and *kombu*.

Most of the seaweed available in the UK is in a cleaned, dried and packaged form. This makes it ideal for storage and it will keep almost indefinitely unopened and for two or three months in an airtight container once opened. Soaking is needed to soften the dehydrated seaweeds and they will then expand by between three and five times their original bulk. Soaking times will be given on the packet but often they are shorter than five minutes. Keep excess soaking water for use in the cooking pot. Cut dried seaweeds with scissors and soaked varieties with a sharp knife. Sea vegetables are best used often in small amounts rather than in large portions infrequently. In this way the body can more efficiently assimilate the concentrated source of nutrients they provide.

If you have a source of fresh seaweed, collect it, wash it in clear running water and store in the refrigerator. It will keep for two to three days. You can also dry it for longer storage periods by hanging it in the sun or a warm dry place.

Nori
This is the most popular of seaweeds. It is known as laver in the West. *Nori* is usually sold in dried sheet form in packets of ten paper-thin sheets, 8 in (20cm) square. It is toasted before use to bring out the flavour and fragrance. To toast a sheet, pass one side over a gas flame a few times until it becomes crisp. It will then crumble easily between thumb and forefinger so that you can sprinkle it over the food. Sheet *nori* is also available ready toasted. It is then called *sushi nori*. *Nori* is most often used to wrap other foods, especially rice, and for crumbling over rice, soups and other dishes as a condiment.

Kombu
Kombu is highly valued in Japan for its iodine content and for its intestinal cleaning and strengthening qualities. There are many varieties and there are even shops in Japan that specialize only in *kombu* products. In the West it is most readily available packaged in convenient strips. Its most common culinary use is in the preparation of stocks. *Kombu* is often covered in a whitish powder; this is just crystallized salt rising to the surface and can be removed by wiping with a dry or slightly damp cloth. *Kombu* needs quite a lot of soaking and cooking if it is not to be used directly in a soup that will be simmered. It has a sweet, pleasing flavour.

Wakame
Wakame is a fringed, dark-green seaweed that thrives in quick-moving ocean currents. It is especially rich in calcium, B vitamins and vitamin C. It is harvested in Japan in the spring and during that season fresh *wakame* is a regular sight on vegetable market stalls. The dried variety looks similar to *kombu* but once soaked it unfurls into a characteristic frond shape with a firm spine or midriff section. This part is removed after soaking by careful cutting if it is tough or if the seaweed is to be used in a delicate dish. *Wakame* is a pleasing colour with an appealing taste and is delicious in soups and salads.

Hijiki

Hijiki is an extremely concentrated source of nutrients and Japanese women endow it with almost magical qualities of enhancing beauty and longevity. It has quite a strong flavour but is used in only small amounts and also sweetens with cooking. Once properly soaked, *hijiki* may be boiled, steamed, sautéed, or added, uncooked, to salads. In their book, *Cooking With Sea Vegetables* (Thorsons £5.99) Peter and Montse Bradford recommend the following methods of soaking: place the *hijiki* in a bowl, cover with water and stir. Then remove the *hijiki* to a second bowl and repeat with fresh water. Repeat again, this time using a cooking pot and the correct amount of water for soaking, as stated in the recipe. Leave to soak for 10 minutes. As with other sea vegetables the water from soaking can be used in cooking but if it is too salty, dilute by adding some fresh water.

Soya Products

Miso

A fermented soya bean and grain product, this has a thick consistency and is usually dark coloured with a pungent smell. Miso is rich in vitamins (including B12) and minerals and is good for settling the digestive system. It can be used in soups, stews, stocks, sauces, dressings, dips and spreads, but it is salty and extra salt should not be necessary. Miso keeps unrefrigerated for months.

Soya Milk

This is made from boiled, crushed soya beans, and used by vegans in place of cow's milk. It is high in protein and low in fat. Soya milk is available in health- and wholefood stores and is also now stocked by some supermarkets. Buy fresh milk in cartons rather than canned milk. Plamil is a well-known brand, but there are many others. Each has a slightly different flavour so it's worth trying a few to find one you like.

Soya Sauce

Soya sauce (*shoyu* in Japanese) is familiar to all Chinese restaurant patrons, although unfortunately the liquid normally found in bottles under this name is a chemically flavoured product which bears little relationship to the real thing. Natural soya sauce is made from a mixture of soya beans, wheat (or barley) and salt, fermented together for up to two years. The resultant mash is pressed and filtered, and the extracted liquid is heated rapidly to seal in the flavour and stop further fermentation. Make sure when you buy soya sauce that you choose one of the natural, fermented varieties. When you use soya sauce be careful not to add too much salt as well, since soya sauce is itself salty.

Tofu (beancurd)

Tofu is a soya bean product commonly used throughout the Far East. It is made from the liquid extracted from crushed soya beans and is a valuable source of minerals, protein and carbohydrate. Beancurd is now generally available in the UK from Chinese grocery stores, health-food shops and some supermarkets. Soft in texture, it is usually sold in packeted small square slabs or loose. It will keep for two or three days in the refrigerator, if covered with water. Cut into cubes and added to soups, vegetable or salad dishes, it is delicious. Fried beancurd is also available. It has a firm yellow crust and can be used in cooked dishes in which fresh beancurd would break up. Silken tofu has a creamy texture and is good for making dressings, dips and creams.

Homemade Beancurd

1 lb (450g) soya beans
3 tablespoons fresh lemon juice

Cover the soya beans with water and leave to soak for at least 12 hours. Change the water once during soaking. Drain the beans and grind them in either an electric grinder or a hand mill. Transfer to a heavy pot and add 2½ times as much water by volume as beans. Bring to the boil, reduce the heat and simmer for 1 hour. Arrange 3 to 4 layers of cheesecloth inside a colander placed over a large pan. Strain the contents of the pan through this. Finally, gather the cheesecloth around the collected pulp and squeeze out as much of the remaining liquid into the pan as possible. Transfer the collected liquid to a glass bowl. Add the lemon juice to it, stir once, cover with a damp cloth and leave in a warm spot (120°F (80°C) is perfect) for 8 to 12 hours or until the beancurd sets. Drain through cheesecloth to remove excess liquid. The beancurd may now be used. For a professional look, pour it into a square mould, put a light weight on top and press for 4 hours. Store under water in a refrigerator.

For flavoured beancurd, simmer a block of it or small squares for 4 to 5 minutes in oil and soya sauce with mint, garlic, nutmeg, cinnamon, cloves, fennel, black pepper, or whatever seasoning you wish.

Pressed Tofu

Pressed tofu may be fried more easily than the tender, fresh, unpressed curd and is less likely to break up in dishes that require long cooking.

To press tofu, lay the cakes of tofu on a wooden chopping board. Place a few sheets of kitchen paper on top and then place a plate or flat dish over them. Weight the dish with a cup of water or a scales weight. Finally, tilt the board slightly (rest one end on an upturned saucer) and leave to drain for one or two hours. The beancurd will then be pressed and ready to use.

Tempeh

Tempeh is a very nutritious fermented soya bean product from Indonesia. The beans are split and parboiled and then a culture is added. The mixture is wrapped into individual portions in leaves or plastic bags and fermented for a day or two. The beans are bound together by the action of the culture and a soft white skin, similar to that on Brie, forms over the surface. The finished tempeh has a nutty taste and it can be cubed and added to other dishes or fried and served on its own. Tempeh is sold in slabs about ⅓ in (0.75cm) to 1½ in (4cm) thick. It is now available in the UK in good health-food stores.

Tahini

A paste made from crushed sesame seeds, used in salad dressings and dips.

Vegetable and Fruit Juices

Raw vegetable and fruit juices provide an excellent way of obtaining the nutrients of fruits and vegetables in a quick, convenient and concentrated form. Juices are rich in vitamins, minerals, enzymes and natural sugars and they are easily assimilated by the bloodstream. Carrot and celery juices are good staple ingredients and they are useful for combining with other stronger-tasting vegetable juices that do not taste so appetizing on their own. Pineapples, pears and apples serve the same role in the preparation of fruit juices. Among many others the following juice combinations are both nutritious and tasty: carrot and apple; carrot and tomato; carrot and celery; orange and pineapple; papaya and pineapple; orange and grapefruit; carrot, apple and lettuce (in 5:3:1 proportions).

For juicing use only fresh, ripe fruits and vegetables. Wash produce thoroughly before use and peel root vegetables, apples and cucumbers. Make only as much juice as you immediately need, since its goodness is lost rapidly through oxidation.

The best juices are those made as needed on your own juicer. There are three types of electric juicer available. The first is as an attachment to a food processor. It works well and, if you already own a food processor, it is the cheapest. The second is an electric juicer in which the residual pulp from the fruit or vegetable remains in the juicing chamber from which the juice is poured. This is perfectly satisfactory but you have to clean it out between each operation. The third and most expensive type is an electric juicer that separates the pulp into one container while the juice flows into another. This is the best type if you plan to make a lot of juices, but it does lose some of the juice with the pulp.

BASICS

Stock

Stockpots were once a constant feature of most busy kitchens. Nowadays, with refrigeration, there is no need to maintain an ongoing stockpot but, particularly during the winter months when soup is a popular part of mealtimes and the kitchen tends to be in use a lot, it still makes sense to prepare your own stock. You save money and provide yourself with a nutritious and tasty base for any soup you wish to make.

Leftover vegetable cuttings may be collected and stored in an airtight container in the refrigerator until you have enough to make a stock. You simply put the vegetables in a pot, cover with about twice their volume in water, season, bring to the boil and simmer for about an hour. Strain and store in the refrigerator, or freeze.

The flavour of the stock varies according to which vegetables you use. Sweet-flavoured ingredients such as parsnips and carrots give a sweet stock, and strongly flavoured greens such as cauliflower or Brussels sprouts need to be used sparingly. Potatoes thicken the broth. Almost any vegetable offcuts may be used, including washed peelings (from organic vegetables) and onion skins. If you wish you may add herbs and spices to the simmering stock for more flavour. Use the prepared stock as a base for soups, sauces and gravies, or even as a hot drink.

The following recipe is for a basic vegetable stock. It can be varied according to your preference and what is available, but gives a general idea of the method.

BASIC VEGETABLE STOCK

1 onion, roughly chopped
2 celery bases or coarse outer
    sticks, roughly chopped
2 medium carrots, roughly
    chopped
1 small turnip, roughly
    chopped (optional)
1 squeezed lemon shell
    (optional)
Leek trimmings (optional)
1 bay leaf
2 sprigs fresh thyme
1 bundle parsley stalks
1 teaspoon whole black
    peppercorns
3 pints (1.75 litres) cold water

Place all the ingredients in a stockpot. Bring to the boil on full heat, reduce heat and simmer for about 1 hour. Strain and use, or leave to cool and store in the refrigerator.

Pastry

Both the pastry recipes given below use partly or wholly wholemeal (wholewheat) flour but if you wish you may substitute plain white flour. If you prefer brown, buy fine-milled wholemeal flour or sieve the coarse milled variety before use. The bran you collect in the sieve may be added to a muesli mix or returned to the main body of the flour.

WHOLEWHEAT SHORTCRUST PASTRY

6 oz (175g) wholewheat flour,
    or 3 oz (75g) plain white
    flour and 3 oz (75g)
    wholewheat flour
¼ teaspoon salt
2½ oz (90g) vegetable
    margarine
Iced water

Makes 10 oz (275g)

Mix the flour and salt together in a bowl. Rub in the margarine until the mixture resembles bread crumbs. Add enough water to form a dough (about 2 fl oz (50ml). If not using the dough immediately cover with a damp cloth and store in the refrigerator.

FLAKY PASTRY

7 oz (200g) wholemeal flour, or substitute plain white flour for part of the wholemeal flour
4 oz (100g) hard vegetable margarine at room temperature
1 teaspoon lemon juice
¼ pt (150ml) cold water

Makes 1 lb (450g)

Sieve the flour into a bowl and add any bran left in the sieve back to the flour. Rub in 1 oz (25g) of the margarine. Add the lemon juice and water and mix to a soft dough. Roll the dough out into an oblong shape, ½ in (1.25cm) thick. Dot 1 oz (25g) margarine, cut into knobs over two-thirds of the pastry. Fold the uncovered third over and then the remaining third on top of that. Use the rolling pin to seal the edges. Turn the dough one turn to the left, roll it into a ½ in (1.25cm) thick oblong again and then repeat the dotting-with-margarine-and-folding process. Cover and rest the pastry in the fridge for 10 minutes. Repeat the rolling, dotting and folding procedure three more times, the last two times without any addition of margarine. Leave the pastry covered in the fridge until ready for use.

Salad Dressings

Other recipes for dressings can be found in the Salads chapter, alongside the recipes in which they are required.

BASIC VINAIGRETTE DRESSING

Do not make your vinaigrette dressing always in the same manner, regardless of what it is going to dress. Heavy dried bean or starchy root vegetable salads may be best with a vinaigrette dressing with a 3:1 oil/vinegar ratio, strongly flavoured greens best with a 4:1

*oil/vinegar ratio, while sweet, delicate lettuce is best with a 5:1 ratio.
A light olive oil is best but its flavour would be wasted if you were
going to add strong spices to the dressing. In that case use peanut or
sunflower oil instead. Mustard is the most usual addition to the basic
vinaigrette. It serves a two-fold purpose; first to give a 'bite' when
used with rich or slightly sweet foods like avocados or root
vegetables, and secondly it helps to emulsify it so that the dressing
clings to the salad instead of running off. If you are going to add
chopped fresh herbs to the vinaigrette add them just before you dress
the salad.*

4½ fl oz (120ml) vegetable oil
2 tablespoons wine vinegar,
  cider vinegar or lemon juice
Salt and freshly ground black
  pepper to taste
1 teaspoon prepared mustard
  (optional)

Makes ¼ pint (150ml)

Place all the ingredients in a bowl or
liquidizer and beat or blend well.
Taste, and adjust the seasoning if
necessary.

TOFU MAYONNAISE

*If you are unfamiliar with tofu see page 22. It is readily available in
health- and wholefood stores and Chinese grocery shops.*

6 oz (175g) fresh tofu, drained
1 tablespoon chopped onion
1 tablespoon olive oil or other
  vegetable oil
1 tablespoon water
1 teaspoon lemon juice
1 teaspoon honey
Salt to taste

Makes about 8 fl oz (225ml)

Place all the ingredients in a liquidizer
or food processor and blend at high
speed. Adjust the seasoning to taste.

Note For different flavours try adding
one or more of the following: crushed
garlic, mustard, chives, tarragon or
dill. Cider vinegar may be used in
place of lemon juice. Silken tofu gives
a thinner mayonnaise than the firmer,
regular variety.

Sauces

Other sauce recipes occur throughout this book alongside the dishes that
they accompany.

WHITE SAUCE

1 oz (25g) vegetable margarine
1 oz (25g) wholemeal flour
1 pint (550ml) soya milk
Sea salt to taste

Makes 1 pint (550ml)

Melt the margarine in a saucepan over a low heat. Take the pan off the heat and stir in the flour. Return to the heat and cook for 5 minutes, stirring occasionally, to make a roux. Set aside. In a separate pan warm up the soya milk. Return the roux to a medium heat and add a little soya milk. Stir with a wooden spoon until smooth. Continue adding small amounts of soya milk until it has all been used. Stir continuously. Bring to a gentle simmer. Add salt to taste.

Note For a low-fat sauce, warm the milk, put it into a liquidizer with the flour and blend for 1 minute. Pour this mixture into a saucepan and bring to the boil, whisking constantly. Turn the heat down to simmer and continue to cook for 5 minutes.

RAW TOMATO SAUCE

Use good, fresh, ripe tomatoes for this sauce.

1 lb (450g) ripe tomatoes, skinned and seeded (see below)
1 tablespoon wine vinegar
2 tablespoons olive oil
1 tablespoon finely chopped fresh parsley
1 teaspoon dried oregano
Salt and freshly ground black pepper to taste

Makes ½ pint (275ml)

Place all the ingredients in a liquidizer and blend at low speed until a smooth sauce is obtained. Serve the sauce over delicate vegetables.

Note For a very quick sauce use tinned tomatoes in place of the fresh ones.

To skin and seed tomatoes
Bring a pan of water to the boil. Take the tomatoes and, with a sharp, pointed knife, remove the stalk and the hard little section of flesh the stalk is attached to. Drop the tomatoes one or two at a time into the boiling water for several seconds. Remove them with a slotted spoon and cool under cold water. The tomato skin will easily peel or even fall off. Cut the tomatoes in half horizontally and squeeze gently to remove excess liquid and seeds.

TOMATO SAUCE

---

2 fl oz (50ml) vegetable oil
1 medium onion, finely diced
2 lb (900g) tinned tomatoes, drained
4 cloves garlic, crushed
1 medium green pepper, cored, seeded and diced
2 teaspoons crushed oregano
2 tablespoons chopped fresh parsley
1 bay leaf
Salt and freshly ground black pepper to taste

Makes about 1½ pints (825ml)

Pour the oil into a heavy saucepan and fry the onion over a low heat until soft. Chop the tomatoes into small pieces and add them, with the garlic and green pepper, to the onion. Stir well and simmer for 10 minutes. Add the herbs and season to taste with salt and black pepper. Simmer for a further 10 minutes.

Variation
For a thicker tomato sauce suitable for pizza toppings or stuffed vegetable and pasta dishes, add 6 oz (175g) tomato purée with the chopped tomatoes.

SOUPS

This chapter contains good, practical but slightly unusual soup recipes from several different countries. There are soups for each season, including chilled soups in the welcome event of a hot summer and some winter soups that can double up as delicious main course dishes. A recipe for vegetable stock is given on page 26, or you could use a vegetable stock cube and water as a substitute.

PADDY'S WINTER VEGETABLE SOUP

Here is a basic recipe for mixed winter vegetable soup, or potate bonne femme as it might be written on some menus. The recipe is not an exact one; half the vegetables are generally potatoes, one quarter onions or sometimes leeks, and the remaining quarter carrots or a mixture of carrots, turnips and celery.

1oz (25g) vegetable margarine
9oz (250g) onions, thinly sliced
7oz (200g) carrots, thinly sliced (optional)
1 stick celery, thinly sliced (optional)
1lb (450g) potatoes, cut into small dice
Bouquet garni (parsley stalks, bay leaf, sprig of thyme)
Salt and freshly ground black pepper to taste

Serves 4

Melt the margarine in a large pan, add the onions and cook uncovered over a low heat until quite soft. Add the carrots and, if using them, the turnip and celery. Stir well and cook for 1 or 2 minutes. Add the diced potato, stir, then add enough water to cover the vegetables by about ½in (1.25cm). Add the bouquet garni and salt, cover and turn up the heat. Once boiling, reduce the heat to a slow simmer and cook for 20 minutes or until the vegetables are soft. Add black pepper to taste, adjust the salt and remove the herbs. Allow the soup to cool slightly before beating it with a wooden spoon or, if you prefer, blending in a liquidizer.

LETTUCE AND TARRAGON SOUP

A good summer soup when lettuce is abundant and a light, herb-flavoured soup suits the warmth of the days.

½ large lettuce, such as iceberg
1 medium onion, finely chopped
2oz (50g) vegetable margarine
1 clove garlic, crushed
1oz (25g) plain flour
1¼ pints (700ml) vegetable stock (see page 26)
1 tablespoon chopped fresh tarragon, or 1 teaspoon dried tarragon
Salt and freshly ground black pepper to taste
¼ pint (150ml) soya yoghurt
Few tarragon leaves to garnish

Serves 4

Shred the lettuce finely (keep back 2 or 3 tablespoons of the shredded centre leaves for garnish). Fry the onion gently in the margarine for 3 to 4 minutes, add the garlic and flour and stir over the heat for 1 minute. Gradually stir in the stock and bring to the boil. Add the shredded lettuce, tarragon, and salt and black pepper to taste. Simmer for 20 minutes. Blend the soup in a liquidizer until smooth. Return to a clean pan and heat through. Add the soya yoghurt and reserved shredded lettuce and heat through, stirring. Do not let the soup boil. Serve piping hot garnished with fresh tarragon.

Note If using dried tarragon, garnish with watercress.

CHESTNUT SOUP

A thick soup with a real country flavour. Tinned chestnuts and chickpeas can be used for this soup.

11oz (300g) tinned chestnuts (or 5oz (150g) dried chestnuts, soaked overnight)
7oz (200g) tinned chickpeas (or 4oz (100g) dried chickpeas, soaked overnight)
4oz (100g) mushrooms, chopped
1 onion, chopped
2 cloves garlic, finely chopped

Drain and mix the chestnuts and chickpeas thoroughly. Fry the mushrooms, onion and garlic in the oil until lightly coloured. Add the tomatoes and stir for 1 or 2 minutes. Add the drained chestnuts and chickpeas. Cover with water, add the stock cube and the chilli and simmer gently, covered for 1 hour (2 hours if dried chestnuts and chickpeas are

2 tablespoons olive oil
7oz (200g) tinned tomatoes
1 vegetable stock cube
1 small dried chilli, crushed
Salt to taste
3 tablespoons finely chopped
    fresh parsley

Serves 4

used). Season with salt after 1 hour – or after the chickpeas have begun to soften, if using dried chickpeas. The chestnuts should break down and thicken the soup. Add more salt, if necessary, and the chopped parsley before serving.

FOUR-FRUITS SOUP

Four-fruits soup is a sweet Chinese dish in which the four main ingredients each have a different shape and texture.

2 oz (50g) pearl barley
14 dried red dates (see note
    below)
1 oz (25g) glutinous or
    pudding rice
3 oz (75g) mung beans,
    soaked overnight and
    drained
3 pints (1.6 litres) water
Sugar to taste

Serves 4

Soak the barley, red dates and rice separately for 3 hours in cold water, rinse well and drain. Remove the stones from the dates and chop into small pieces. Put the barley, dates, rice and mung beans into a pan with the water and boil gently for 1½ hours. Add sugar to taste and serve either hot or cold.

Note There is a wide range of preserved and dried fruits available from China and Taiwan, including crystallized white melon, 'dehydrated' papaya and pineapple, preserved kumquats, apples, plums and red dates without stones; none of these need soaking before use. There are also dried red and black dates which need soaking for several hours before use.

TURKISH ONION SOUP

Onion soup is popular in Iran and Turkey as well as in France. Its preparation is similar to French onion soup, but the seasoning is different.

2 fl oz (50ml) olive oil
1 lb (450g) onions, thinly
  sliced
2½ pints (1.4 litres) water
1 oz (25g) wholemeal flour
Salt and freshly ground black
  pepper to taste
½ teaspoon turmeric
1 teaspoon sugar
Juice of 1 lemon
2 teaspoons dried mint
½ teaspoon ground cinnamon
4 to 6 slices French bread

Serves 4 to 6

Heat the oil in a heavy pan and add the onions. Cook for 15 minutes over a gentle heat, stirring occasionally. Use a little of the water to make a paste with the flour and stir this into the onions. Stirring constantly, continue to cook the onion and flour mixture for 2 to 3 minutes. Add the remaining water and bring to the boil. Reduce the heat and season to taste with salt and black pepper. Add the turmeric, sugar and lemon juice, cover and leave to simmer for 45 minutes or longer. Adjust the seasoning to taste, if necessary. Rub the mint to a powder and mix with the cinnamon. Stir this mixture into the soup and remove from the heat. Lightly toast the slices of French bread, put one piece each in individual serving bowls, pour in the soup and serve.

SPICY CARROT AND ORANGE SOUP

An unusual combination of carrot, orange and ginger. Serve either hot or well chilled.

1 oz (25g) vegetable margarine
1 lb (450g) carrots, roughly
  chopped
1 medium onion, chopped
1 clove garlic, crushed
1 teaspoon grated ginger root
  or ¼ teaspoon ground
  ginger

Melt the margarine in a saucepan and add the carrots and onion. Cook for 5 minutes and then add the garlic, ginger, stock, orange juice and almost all the rind. Bring to the boil, reduce the heat and simmer for 15 minutes or until the carrots are very tender. Blend

1 pint (550ml) vegetable stock (see page 26)
Juice of 2 oranges and grated rind of ½ orange
Salt and freshly ground black pepper to taste

Serves 4

in a liquidizer until smooth then return the soup to the pan. Reheat and season to taste with salt and black pepper. Serve garnished with the remaining grated orange rind.

WATERCRESS SOUP

This is a simple but nutritious Chinese soup.

1¾ pints (1 litre) vegetable stock (see page 26)
¼ teaspoon salt
1 tablespoon soya sauce
1 teaspoon sugar
1 teaspoon grated ginger root
2 bunches watercress – remove thick stems and discard, divide the rest into sprigs
2 spring onions, finely chopped

Serves 4

Combine the stock, salt, soya sauce, sugar and ginger in a saucepan and bring to the boil. Reduce the heat, cover and simmer for 15 minutes. Return to a fast boil and add the watercress and spring onions. Simmer for a further 2 to 3 minutes and serve immediately.

SPINACH AND GINGER SOUP

This is a tasty and quick-to-prepare Indonesian soup. Chinese leaves or watercress may be substituted for the spinach.

2 tablespoons vegetable oil
1 in (2.5cm) piece ginger root, finely chopped
1 oz (25g) raw peanuts, dry-roasted (see page 18) and crushed, or 1½ teaspoons crunchy peanut butter
1½ pints (825ml) water or vegetable stock (see page 26), boiling

Heat the oil in a saucepan, add the ginger and stir-fry it gently for 2 minutes. Add the crushed peanuts or peanut butter and stir-fry for 1 minute. Pour in the boiling water or stock, add the spinach and simmer, covered, for 5 minutes. In a small bowl combine the cornflour, turmeric, soya sauce, sugar, salt and pepper, and

10 oz (275g) fresh spinach,
  finely chopped
1 teaspoon cornflour
½ teaspoon ground turmeric
1 tablespoon soya sauce
½ teaspoon dark brown sugar
Salt and freshly ground black
  pepper to taste

Serves 4

2 tablespoons of stock from the soup.
Make the mixture into a paste and stir
this into the soup, leaving it to
simmer, covered, for a further 10
minutes. Adjust the seasoning to taste,
and serve.

Variation
To pep up the soup in the Indonesian
manner add 1 or 2 finely chopped
chilli peppers when you cook the
ginger.

RED BEAN AND SPINACH SOUP

*This is a rich and nourishing soup which may be served as a main
meal.*

8 oz (225g) red beans, soaked
  overnight and drained
4 tablespoons vegetable oil
2 medium onions, diced
½ teaspoon ground turmeric
Pinch of cayenne
8 oz (225g) red, brown or
  green lentils, washed and
  drained
4 oz (100g) brown or white
  rice, washed and drained
3 pints (1.75 litres) water
Salt and freshly ground black
  pepper to taste
1 lb (450g) fresh spinach,
  washed and chopped
Juice of 2 lemons

Serves 4

Put the beans in a heavy pot, add 1
pint (550ml) water, and cook until just
tender (about 1 hour). You may need
to add more water during cooking.
Transfer the beans and cooking liquid
to another container, clean the pot out
and add the vegetable oil. Add the
onions and sauté over a moderate heat
until just brown. Stir in the turmeric,
cayenne, lentils and rice and sauté,
stirring, for a further minute or two.
Pour in the water and the reserved
beans with their cooking liquid.
Season to taste with salt and black
pepper and bring to the boil. Reduce
the heat, cover and simmer for 45
minutes. Now add the spinach and
more turmeric and cayenne if needed.
Return to the boil, reduce the heat,
cover and simmer for a further 15
minutes. Stir in the lemon juice, leave
for 2 or 3 minutes on the heat, and
then serve.

BUTTER BEAN SOUP

Nowadays beans such as red beans or chickpeas are very popular but old standbys such as butter beans should not be forgotten.

4 oz (100g) butter beans, soaked overnight
2 sticks celery, chopped
2 large carrots, sliced
2 small leeks, sliced
1 medium onion, chopped
¼ teaspoon dried thyme
Pinch of cayenne pepper
1 bay leaf
Salt and freshly ground black pepper to taste
¼ pint (150ml) soya milk (optional)
2 fl oz (50ml) soya yoghurt

Serves 4

Drain the beans and put them into a saucepan with 1 pint (550ml) fresh water. Bring to the boil, add the celery, carrots, leeks, onion, thyme, cayenne pepper and bay leaf. Cover and simmer for 45 minutes, or until the beans are tender. Blend the soup until smooth, return to the rinsed saucepan. Add salt and black pepper to taste and thin to the desired consistency with soya milk if you wish, or use boiling water. Heat through, stir in the soya yoghurt and serve.

POTATO AND BROCCOLI SOUP

Winter greens and root vegetables make a nutritious combination and they can provide the extra vitamins and minerals we need during cold, sunless months. This soup simply uses two of the most readily available green and root vegetables.

1 small onion, finely chopped
1 oz (25g) vegetable margarine
1 lb (450g) potatoes, cut into ¾ in (2cm) cubes
1 oz (25g) wholemeal flour
1¼ pints (700ml) vegetable stock (see page 26) or water
Salt and freshly ground black pepper to taste
8 oz (225g) broccoli, divided into small florets

Serves 4

Fry the onion gently in the margarine for 3 minutes. Add the cubed potatoes and fry for a further minute. Stir in the flour and cook for 30 seconds. Gradually stir in the stock or water and bring to the boil. Add seasoning to taste and simmer for 10 to 15 minutes (or 20 minutes if using water instead of stock). Now, if you have not used stock, stir the soup well with a wooden spoon to break up the potato and enhance the flavour. Add the broccoli and simmer for a further 4 or

5 minutes until just tender. Serve.

Note This gives a textured soup; for a smoother soup, blend in a liquidizer or food processor then reheat.

MISO AND VEGETABLE SOUP

Miso soup is rich in vitamins and minerals and is also good for the digestive system. It is popular in Japan, where it is often served with rice for breakfast.

2 tablespoons vegetable oil
4 oz (100g) white radish (daikon) or young turnips, finely chopped into matchsticks
1 small onion, finely chopped
4 oz (100g) courgettes, thinly sliced
2 oz (50g) mushrooms, sliced
2 to 3 oz (50 to 75g) miso, to taste
2 pints (1.1 litres) water
Sprigs of parsley to garnish, or 1 sheet of *nori* seaweed, toasted and crumbled (see page 20)

Serves 4

Heat the oil in a heavy pan and sauté the white radish or turnip, onion and carrots until just softened. Stir in the mushrooms and sauté for a further minute or two. Cream the miso with a little of the water and add the remaining water to the pan. Bring to the boil and stir in the creamed miso. Return the soup to a low boil and simmer until the vegetables are cooked. Serve garnished with parsley sprigs or crumbled nori.

Note Other vegetables may be used in this recipe – for example, you could use potatoes in place of the daikon or turnips.

CABBAGE AND CORIANDER SOUP

This Thai-inspired soup is quick to make and tasty.

1 tablespoon vegetable oil
2 cloves garlic, crushed
½ teaspoon coriander seeds, ground
¼ teaspoon freshly ground black pepper

Heat the oil in a large saucepan and stir in the garlic, coriander and black pepper. Stir-fry until the garlic just turns golden. Add the soya sauce and stock and bring to a low simmer. Simmer for 10 minutes then add the

2 teaspoons soya sauce
2 pints (1.1 litres) vegetable
  stock (see page 00)
12 oz (350g) cabbage, finely
  shredded
2 spring onions, finely
  chopped
1 tablespoon finely chopped
  fresh coriander leaves
½ fresh or dried red chilli
  pepper, seeded and thinly
  sliced (optional)

Serves 4

cabbage. Return to the boil, then reduce the heat and simmer for 7 minutes or until the cabbage is tender. Serve immediately, garnished with the chopped spring onions, coriander leaves and, if you like hot food, chilli pepper rings as well.

CELERY AND ALMOND SOUP

Almonds are a good ingredient in soups. They have a nutty but sweet flavour, blend well and give a milky texture.

1 oz (25g) vegetable margarine
1 medium onion, chopped
¾ head celery, cleaned and
  chopped – reserve a few
  leaves for garnish
1 bay leaf
1 medium potato, chopped
2 oz (50g) blanched almonds,
  lightly dry-roasted (see page
  18) – reserve a few for
  garnish
1¼ pints (700ml) vegetable
  stock (see page 26) or water
Salt and freshly ground black
  pepper

Serves 4

Heat the margarine in a saucepan and sauté the onion for 2 to 3 minutes until softened. Add the celery, stir, and sauté for a further 3 minutes. Add the bay leaf, potato, almonds, stock or water and salt and black pepper to taste. Bring to the boil, cover, then reduce the heat and simmer for 20 to 25 minutes. Remove the bay leaf and blend the soup in a liquidizer until smooth. Return to the rinsed pan and reheat. Serve garnished with the reserved celery leaves and almonds.

TUSCAN HARICOT BEAN SOUP

This soup requires a little advance planning but once the beans have been soaked it can be quickly put together and then left to cook.

2 tablespoons vegetable oil
2 cloves garlic, crushed
1 medium onion, sliced
1 carrot, chopped
2 stalks celery and their leaves, chopped
8 oz (225g) tinned tomatoes
1 teaspoon finely chopped dried rosemary
¼ teaspoon chilli powder or hot pepper sauce
8 oz (225g) haricot beans, soaked overnight then drained
2 pints (1.1 litres) water
Salt and freshly ground black pepper to taste

Serves 4 to 6

Heat the oil in a heavy saucepan and sauté the garlic and onion until just softened. Add the carrot and celery and sauté until the onion is browned. Stir in the tomatoes, rosemary and chilli powder or hot pepper sauce. Add the haricot beans and water and bring to the boil. Reduce the heat, cover and simmer for 1½ to 2 hours. With a slotted spoon remove about half the beans and blend in a liquidizer. Return this purée to the pan, season to taste with salt and pepper, and return to the boil. Serve.

Variation
After puréeing half the beans, add 1 oz (25g) spaghetti, broken into 1 in (2.5cm) pieces, to the pot. Bring to the boil and cook until the spaghetti is *al dente* (about 6 minutes). Serve.

LENTIL SOUP

This delicious Middle Eastern version of lentil soup is served topped with fried garlic and onions and accompanied by fresh lemon wedges.

12 oz (350g) lentils (red, brown or green), washed
2½ pints (1.4 litres) water or vegetable stock (see page 26)
1 medium onion, finely diced
1 medium carrot, sliced
1 teaspoon ground cumin
Juice of 1 lemon

Put the lentils in a heavy pot with the water or stock, add the onion and carrot and bring to the boil. Reduce the heat, cover and simmer for 1 hour or until the lentils are very soft. Blend the mixture in a liquidizer or push it through a sieve. Return it to the pot and add the cumin, lemon juice, and

Salt and freshly ground black
pepper to taste
2 tablespoons olive oil
2 cloves garlic, crushed
1 large onion, thinly sliced
1 lemon, cut into wedges

Serves 4

salt and black pepper to taste. Return
to a gentle simmer for 15 minutes.
Meanwhile, heat the oil in a frying
pan and sauté the garlic for a minute
or two. Add the onion and fry until
golden brown. Serve the soup in bowls
and top each one with a portion of the
browned onions and garlic. Serve a
side dish of lemon wedges for extra
juice.

Chilled Soups

Chilled soup is delicious on a warm evening or, on cooler nights, served
as a refreshing starter to a hot main dish. Remember, however, that a
chilled soup needs to be more strongly flavoured than if served hot.

CUCUMBER AND CHIVE SOUP

This gentle, refreshing soup can be served hot or cold.

1 small onion, finely chopped
½ cucumber, finely diced
1 oz (25g) vegetable margarine
1 oz (25g) wholemeal flour
1 pint (550ml) vegetable stock
(see page 26)
¼ pint (150ml) soya milk
2 tablespoons finely chopped
fresh chives
Salt and freshly ground black
pepper to taste

Serves 4

Fry the onion and most of the
cucumber (reserve a little for garnish)
in the margarine until the onion is
softened. Stir in the flour and cook for
a further minute. Add the stock, soya
milk, chives and salt and black pepper
to taste. Simmer for about 15 minutes,
then blend the soup until it is almost
smooth but still has some texture.
Serve hot or cold, garnished with the
reserved diced cucumber.

CHILLED SUMMER VEGETABLE MISO SOUP

1¾ pints (1 litre) vegetable stock (see page 26), chilled
2 to 3 oz (50 to 75g) miso, to taste
4 oz (100g) cucumber, thinly sliced and chilled
4 oz (100g) tomatoes, finely diced and chilled
Small bunch fresh mint, chopped

Serves 4

Blend the stock and miso together. Divide the cucumber and tomatoes between 4 bowls, pour on the soup and garnish with the mint.

CURRIED APPLE SOUP

½ oz (15g) vegetable margarine
1 lb (450g) dessert apples, peeled, cored and chopped, plus 1 dessert apple for garnish
1 medium onion, finely chopped
½ to 1 tablespoon medium curry powder
1 pint (550ml) vegetable stock (see page 26)
Piece of cinnamon stick (optional)
8 fl oz (225ml) soya milk diluted with 4 fl oz (100ml) water
A little lemon juice

Serves 4

Melt the margarine in a large saucepan, add the apple and onion, then cover and cook gently until tender. Add the curry powder and cook over a medium heat, stirring, for 2 or 3 minutes. Pour in the stock and add the cinnamon, if using. Bring to the boil, cover and simmer for 10 minutes, stirring occasionally. Purée the soup in a blender. Allow to cool, then stir in the diluted soya milk. Chill, covered, for 2 hours. Just before serving, stir well and pour into a large serving bowl or individual bowls. Finely chop or slice the reserved apple, toss in lemon juice to prevent discolouration, and use to garnish the soup.

BORSCHT (CHILLED BEETROOT SOUP)

Try this Eastern European soup on a really hot day, when it is very refreshing either as a starter or a meal in itself. Serve it as a sauce, too, with cooked root vegetables or grains.

1 medium onion, chopped
2 tablespoons vegetable oil
1 oz (25g) wholemeal flour
2 or 3 sticks celery, chopped
2 large raw beetroots, chopped
2 teaspoons fresh mixed
  herbs, chopped, or 1
  teaspoon dried mixed herbs
1¾ pints (1 litre) water
1 clove garlic
Soya sauce to taste
2 tablespoons chopped fresh
  parsley
8 oz (225g) tomatoes, or 1
  small can, chopped
4 fl oz (100ml) soya milk
  (optional)

Serves 4 to 6

Sauté the onion in the oil for 5 minutes. Add the flour and stir it in well, then add the celery, beetroot, mixed herbs and water. Stir well and bring to the boil. Reduce the heat, cover and simmer for 45 minutes. Liquidize the contents of the pan in a blender with the garlic, soya sauce, parsley and tomatoes. Pour the soup into a serving dish and chill for at least 5 hours in the fridge. Serve with a swirl of soya milk in each bowl, if liked.

GAZPACHO

A chilled tureen of smooth gazpacho soup surrounded by small bowls of accompanying chopped vegetables makes a splendid centrepiece for an informal meal. The soup can be swiftly prepared in a liquidizer, but it does need to be made at least an hour ahead of serving to give it time to chill and the flavours to mingle.

1½ lb (675g) ripe tomatoes
½ cucumber, roughly chopped
1 red pepper, roughly chopped
4 spring onions, roughly
  chopped
2 cloves garlic, peeled
Juice of ½ small lemon
1 oz (25g) breadcrumbs
4 tablespoons olive oil

Cut the tomatoes in half horizontally, lightly squeeze them to expel the seeds and excess moisture, then chop roughly and place in a liquidizer. Blend until barely smooth. Pour this purée into a mixing bowl and set aside. Place the cucumber, red pepper, spring onions, garlic, lemon juice,

12 black olives, pitted and
  roughly chopped
2 tablespoons chopped fresh
  parsley
2 tablespoons chopped fresh
  chervil
1 tablespoon chopped fresh
  tarragon
12 well-crushed coriander
  seeds
Salt and freshly ground black
  pepper to taste
A few sprigs of chervil to
  garnish

*Suggested accompaniments to
  the soup:*
1 small bowl diced cucumber
1 small bowl diced red and
  green pepper, mixed
1 small bowl finely sliced
  spring onions
1 small bowl finely sliced
  celery
A few black olives, hazelnuts
  or almonds

Serves 6

breadcrumbs, olive oil and olives in
the liquidizer and blend until smooth.
Add this to the tomato purée, stir in
the herbs and the crushed coriander
seeds, season with pepper and salt.
Pour into a serving bowl and set aside
to chill. Garnish with the chervil
sprigs before serving with the small
bowls of accompaniments.

In this collection of starters I have chosen recipes from various cuisines to produce a range of dishes that please the eye and the palate. They may be served as starters in the conventional manner or five or six of them could be served together in the Middle Eastern *mezze* style or as the basis of a buffet meal. Many also make excellent side dishes to a main course.

FLORIDA MELON

This is a versatile recipe which can be served either as a refreshing starter or a pudding.

2 small honeydew melons
1 grapefruit, peeled and
    segmented
2 oranges, peeled and
    segmented
2 oz (50g) roasted peanuts
1 oz (25g) soft brown sugar
¼ teaspoon ground cinnamon

Serves 4

Halve the melons. Scoop out and discard the seeds, then remove and chop the melon flesh. Reserve the melon skin. In a bowl, mix the melon flesh and citrus fruits together. Pile the mixed fruits back into the melon shells. Chop the peanuts and mix with the sugar and cinnamon. Sprinkle this mixture over the fruit and serve.

IMAM BAYELDI (BAKED STUFFED AUBERGINES)

This is a well-known Turkish dish. Its name means the Imam who fainted. It's not known whether he fainted because the dish was so delicious or because he thought his wife was being extravagant making such a rich dish for a humble man of God. Whatever, I hope you can enjoy it without any pangs of conscience. The dish can be served as a starter or as a main meal. In the former case the aubergines are cut into small portions before serving.

2 medium aubergines
4 fl oz (100ml) olive oil
2 medium onions, finely
    chopped
1 medium green pepper,
    seeded and finely chopped

Wash the aubergines and cut the stems off. Cut them lengthwise into halves, and make a deep slit down the centre of each piece. Put the aubergines in a colander, salt them generously and set aside for 30 minutes. Now wash,

2 cloves garlic, chopped
2 tomatoes, chopped
1 bunch parsley, chopped
Salt and freshly ground black
  pepper to taste
Juice of 1 lemon
Tomato sauce (see page 30)
  (optional)

Serves 4

drain and pat them dry. Using a little of the oil, lightly brown each half in a heavy frying pan then remove and set aside. Add half the remaining oil to the frying pan and put in the onions, green pepper and garlic. Sauté and stir the mixture until the onions are nicely softened. Add the tomatoes and parsley and cook for a further 2 to 3 minutes.

Season to taste with salt and black pepper. Arrange the aubergine halves in a casserole and tightly pack the slash in each one with the onion and tomato filling. Sprinkle over the remaining oil and pour into the dish the lemon juice and enough water to come two-thirds of the way up the side of the stuffed aubergines. Cover the dish and simmer gently on the top of the oven for 1 hour or until the aubergines are soft and well cooked. Alternatively, cover the stuffed aubergines with tomato sauce and bake covered in a preheated oven, 375°F (190°C, gas mark 5) for 1 hour. Serve cold.

SPICY LEMON CUCUMBER SALAD

This Southeast Asian salad is excellent as a light, refreshing starter, as a side dish, or as a garnish for main meals, particularly curried dishes. In the Far East it is made from the small, gherkin-type cucumbers sometimes available in the UK from Indian grocery stores. This type of cucumber is used unpeeled and unseeded. Normal cucumbers are also fine for the recipe but they should be peeled and seeded.

2 lb (900g) small gherkin
  cucumbers, finely sliced, or

Combine the cucumber, onion and salt in a bowl and mix well together.

2 medium cucumbers,
peeled, seeded and finely
sliced
1 medium onion, finely sliced
1 tablespoon salt
3 tablespoons lemon juice
¼ teaspoon cayenne pepper
(add more if you like hot
food)
2 tablespoons sesame seeds
1 tablespoon sesame oil
(peanut or sunflower oil
may be used as alternatives)

Serves 4

Set aside for 1 hour and then drain off all the liquid that has formed. Gently press the cucumber and onion to extract more liquid, discard this also. Stir in the lemon juice and cayenne pepper. Dry-roast the sesame seeds (see page 18) until they start to jump in the pan then add them to the bowl together with the sesame oil. Mix well, cover, chill and serve.

AUBERGINE CAVIAR

I once had real caviar and wondered what all the fuss was about. This aubergine 'caviar' is just as tasty.

2 cloves garlic, crushed
3 tablespoons olive oil
1 medium aubergine
1 bunch spring onions, finely
chopped
Salt and freshly ground black
pepper to taste
1 teaspoon cardamom powder
1 teaspoon ground coriander
Black olives and tiny lettuce
leaves (Little Gem) to
garnish

Serves 4

Preheat the oven to 350°F (180°C, gas mark 4). Soak the garlic in the olive oil. Bake the aubergine whole and unpeeled for 40 to 60 minutes, according to size. Test with a skewer or knitting needle; if it is soft all the way through, it is done. Leave to cool, then cut open and scrape away all the pulp from the skin. Mash the pulp with the garlic, olive oil, spring onions, seasoning and spices. Put in an attractive dish and serve garnished with black olives and tiny lettuce leaves.

GREEN APPLES WITH SWEET HOT SAUCE

In Thailand this dish would be made with green mangoes so if they are available substitute them for the apples. Otherwise use crisp, only slightly sweet apples, like Granny Smiths. Serving apples in this way usually causes a surprise. People are not used to seeing them in such strange company.

4 crisp green apples, cored
   and sliced into 6 pieces each
1 teaspoon lemon juice
3 tablespoons soya sauce
4 oz (100g) white sugar
¼ to ½ teaspoon chilli sauce
1 tablespoon finely diced
   onion

Serves 4

Put the apples in a bowl of water to which the lemon juice has been added and put them in the fridge to chill slightly (15 to 30 minutes). Put the soya sauce and sugar in a small pan and heat gently until the sugar has dissolved. Pour the mixture into a small bowl and set it aside for 10 minutes to cool. Now stir in the chilli sauce and onion. Set the bowl of sauce in the centre of a large plate and arrange the apple slices around it so people can dip them into the sauce.

RED BEAN, LEMON AND OLIVE OIL DIP

A rich, tasty dip. Serve with warm pitta bread.

6 tablespoons olive oil
2 large onions, finely chopped
1 lb (450g) canned red kidney
   beans, drained
5 tablespoons lemon juice
1 teaspoon honey
Salt to taste

Garnish
2 tablespoons olive oil
2 tablespoons lemon juice
3 tablespoons chopped fresh
   parsley
1 teaspoon paprika

Serves 4 to 6

Heat the oil in a pan and sauté the onions until soft (about 5 minutes). Put the onions and oil in a blender with the beans, lemon juice, honey and salt. Liquidize until smooth. Transfer to a serving bowl. Mix the garnish ingredients together and trickle the mixture over the dip. Serve.

HUMMUS BI TAHINI

Hummus is the favourite dip of the Middle East and Greece. Its ingredients do not look that special but when combined they are delicious. An electric blender makes this a quick dip to prepare whereas the manual process is laborious. Serve with warm pitta bread.

1 lb (450g) canned chickpeas
4 fl oz (100ml) olive oil
2 or 3 cloves garlic, peeled
4 fl oz (100ml) lemon juice
¼ pint (150ml) tahini
1 teaspoon salt
Pinch of paprika

Serves 4

Drain the chickpeas, reserving the liquid. Put half of them into a blender and add three-quarters of the oil, the garlic, lemon juice, tahini and salt. Blend at high speed until the mixture is smooth. Add the remaining chickpeas slowly with the blender running. If the mixture gets too thick to turn, add some of the reserved liquid. Finally, taste the hummus and add more salt, lemon juice or garlic if needed. Scrape the hummus into a serving dish, dribble the remaining oil over the top, decorate the centre with a pinch of paprika and serve. Hummus keeps well in the refrigerator for 4 to 5 days.

TRADITIONAL FRENCH CRUDITÉS

Not a single salad but a collection of the very simplest salads mixed with the simplest dressings. Try a selection of the following as a starter or to accompany a light meal.

Raw carrots, scrubbed clean,
  finely grated and dressed
  just with lemon juice.

Raw shelled broad beans
  sprinkled with coarse sea
  salt.

Beetroot, lightly cooked, the
  skins rubbed off, cubed.

RIDER BOOKS

Mailing List

Editorial Department

Random Century House

20 Vauxhall Bridge Road

London SW1V 2SA

PLACE
STAMP
HERE

*If you wish to receive a copy
of the latest Rider catalogue of books
and to be placed on our mailing list
please send us this card.*

PLEASE PRINT

Book in which this card was found

NAME

ADDRESS

CITY

POSTAL CODE   COUNTRY
                     (IF OUTSIDE UK)

Cucumber, peeled, cut into finest rounds, dressed with good white wine vinegar or cider vinegar and left to marinate for 30 minutes.

Peppers, deseeded, cut into thin circles and steeped in olive oil.

Firm tomatoes, sliced, lightly dressed with vinaigrette and sprinkled with freshly ground black pepper and chopped parsley

To serve – various

SKORDHALIA

In her well-known *Vegetable Book* Jane Grigson mentions that skordhalia is the Greek equivalent of *ailloli* (a garlic mayonnaise eaten with bread), but that it is made without egg yolks because by tradition it was eaten at Lent (with boiled beetroot and potatoes). It is also good with vegetable fritters (see page 91).

2 in (5cm)-thick slice of stale white bread, crusts removed
3 or more cloves of garlic, crushed to a paste with salt
4 oz (100g) walnuts, roughly ground
4 fl oz (100ml) olive oil
White wine vinegar
Parsley, olives and sliced lemon to garnish

Serves 4

Soak the bread in cold water for 5 minutes. Then squeeze out the water; the bread will be like a thick paste. Place the bread and the garlic in a blender. Blend, then add the walnuts and blend again until a homogeneous mixture is obtained. Add the olive oil, drop by drop, as for mayonnaise, then more quickly until all the oil is absorbed. The mixture should be creamy. Sharpen to taste with wine vinegar. Transfer to a dish and garnish with parsley, olives and lemon slices.

TOASTED CHICKPEAS AND ALMONDS

If you are using dried chickpeas as opposed to the tinned, cooked variety, they will need to be soaked overnight.

8 oz (225g) chickpeas, covered
  in water, soaked overnight,
  or 1 lb (450g) tinned
  chickpeas, drained
2 tablespoons olive oil
2 cloves garlic, crushed
Salt to taste
12 oz (350g) almonds, not
  skinned

Serves 4

If using dried and soaked chickpeas, cover them with fresh water and bring to the boil. Reduce the heat, cover and simmer for just less than 1 hour or until the chickpeas are almost but not quite tender. Drain the chickpeas (if you wish, reserve the cooking water for use in the preparation of a stock).

Heat half the oil in a heavy frying pan and lightly sauté half the crushed garlic. Add half the chickpeas and gently fry, stirring, over a low heat for 5 minutes. Remove from the pan and set aside. Repeat the process with the remaining oil, garlic and chickpeas then add them to the first batch. Add salt to taste. Preheat the grill and spread the almonds in a single layer on a baking sheet. Toast them under the grill, shaking occasionally, until they begin to turn brown. Combine the chickpeas and almonds and store in an airtight tin. Serve cold or heated through in a medium oven for 10 minutes before serving.

GREEN BEANS IN OIL

Vegetables cooked in oil with lemon juice and tomatoes are a popular Middle Eastern starter. The dish is served lukewarm or cold and consequently olive oil is the best oil to choose. This recipe uses green beans but artichoke hearts are also commonly prepared in this way. Serve with fresh bread.

1 lb (450g) fresh or frozen
  green beans (string beans)
1 medium onion, finely sliced
3 tablespoons olive oil
3 large tomatoes, chopped
2 cloves garlic, crushed
½ teaspoon sugar
Salt and freshly ground black
  pepper to taste
Juice of 1 lemon

Serves 4

Either defrost the beans or wash them
well, top and tail, and where necessary
string them. Cut the beans in half or if
they are very long cut them into 2 in
(5cm) lengths. Sauté the onion in the
oil in a heavy pan until it is just soft,
then add the tomatoes and cook until
they are soft. Add the beans and stir
well. Add the garlic and sugar and
season to taste with salt and black
pepper. Just cover the contents of the
pan with water and simmer for 30
minutes or until the beans are very
tender. Leave them to cool in the pan.
Just before serving, squeeze the lemon
juice over the beans.

POTATO CAKE

*Serve this Mediterranean dish hot or cold as a first course. Serve on
its own or with bread or raw vegetable crudité.*

1 large onion, chopped
2 tablespoons olive oil
12 oz (350g) tinned tomatoes,
  drained and chopped
¼ pint (150ml) dry white
  wine
Salt and freshly ground black
  pepper to taste
1 oz (25g) black olives, stoned
  and roughly chopped
1 lb (450g) potatoes in their
  skins

Serves 4

Fry the onion in the olive oil over a
very low heat until very soft but hardly
coloured, stirring often. Add the
tomatoes and wine. Season with salt
and pepper. Add the olives and
simmer for half an hour or so until
reduced to a thick sauce. In the
meantime, boil the potatoes until soft.
Peel and mash them and add them
gradually to the tomato sauce, letting
each spoonful become absorbed. A
firm, slightly moist texture is what you
want to achieve. Shape into a cake and
serve.

GUACAMOLE

Guacamole is a Mexican spiced avocado sauce which can be used as a dip for raw or parboiled vegetables, or served as a starter with corn tortilla chips or fresh bread.

2 large avocados, the flesh soft but not discoloured
1 beef tomato or 2 large ordinary tomatoes, peeled, deseeded, juiced and chopped (see page 30)
2 tablespoons chopped onion (white of spring onions is best)
1 tablespoon chopped fresh coriander leaves
1 tablespoon lemon juice
1 clove garlic, very finely chopped
1 fresh chilli pepper, deseeded and very finely chopped, or hot pepper sauce to taste
1 teaspoon paprika (optional)
Salt and freshly ground black pepper to taste

Serves 4 to 6

Peel and dice the avocados and turn them into a steep-sided mixing bowl. Add all the other ingredients and mix together, but not so well that all trace of the separate ingredients disappears. Divide the salad between individual plates and serve.

Note Guacamole quickly deteriorates in the air. If you have some left over you can extend its life by almost filling a small container with it and then sealing the top with a thin layer of oil. When you want to serve the gaucamole pour off the excess oil and stir in any oil that remains on the surface.

CELERY AND GREEN PEPPER WITH SESAME SAUCE

This is a light, tasty, Chinese-inspired dish.

2 to 3 sticks celery including leaves, washed
1 large green pepper
2 tablespoons soya sauce
1 tablespoon sesame oil
1 teaspoon brown sugar
8 very thin slivers of fresh peeled ginger root
2 teaspoons sesame seeds, dry-roasted (see page 18)

Serves 4

Cut the celery diagonally into 2 in (5cm) lengths. Reserve the leaves. Cut the pepper in half, core and deseed, cut in half again and then cut each piece into quarters. Heat a pan of slightly salted water to boiling and blanch the celery and pepper pieces for 30 seconds only. Remove and drain. Mix together the soya sauce, sesame oil and brown sugar. Stir this sauce into the vegetables and divide

them between 4 individual plates.
Garnish each plate with a few
chopped celery leaves, slivers of ginger
root and sesame seeds.

Variation
For a sweet-sour sauce add 1
tablespoon lemon juice to the sauce
ingredients.

SICILIAN CAULIFLOWER

This Mediterranean recipe has a wonderful flavour and makes a good starter or light lunch dish.

1 medium cauliflower
4 tablespoons olive oil
1 large onion, chopped
1 large onion, chopped
12 black olives, stoned and
  sliced
½ tablespoon chopped fresh
  rosemary, if available
Salt and freshly ground black
  pepper to taste
¼ pint (150ml) coarse red
  wine

Serves 4

Divide the cauliflower into even-sized
florets. Pour a little of the oil into a
deepish heavy pan with a lid. Add
some of the onion and olives. Add a
layer of cauliflower, a sprinkling of oil
and rosemary, and a very little salt and
pepper. Repeat the layers. Finish by
pouring on the remaining oil with the
red wine. Cover and cook gently until
the cauliflower is tender. The liquid
should have evaporated more or less
by the time the cauliflower is done,
but be prepared to raise the heat to
boil it away. Turn on to a hot serving
dish and serve.

APPLE AND GRAPES WITH JAPANESE MUSTARD

The large black muscat grapes available in early winter and around Christmas are particularly excellent with this salad (other grapes are fine as well), which makes an unusual, appetizing, bitter-sweet starter.

1 teaspoon Japanese *wasabi* mustard or prepared English mustard

2 tablespoons rice vinegar or cider vinegar

1 tablespoon *shoyu* (natural soya sauce)

1 to 2 teaspoons sugar

8 oz (225g) eating apples, cored, cut into small chunks

Juice of ½ lemon

8 oz (225g) large grapes, washed

1 teaspoon mustard seeds

Serves 4

Combine the mustard, vinegar and *shoyu* in a small mixing bowl, add sugar to taste and stir well to dissolve the sugar. Set aside in the refrigerator. Sprinkle the apple chunks with lemon juice and set aside to chill. Cut the grapes in half and pick out the seeds with the tip of a pointed knife. Lightly chill the grapes. Before serving toss the apple and grapes together in the dressing and then divide the salad between individual serving bowls.

DOLMADES (STUFFED VINE LEAVES)

Stuffed vine leaves are a traditional Greek starter. They are excellent cold and can be made the day before needed and then chilled ready for serving.

2 medium onions, finely diced

2 tablespoons olive oil

12 oz (350g) long grain rice, washed and drained

3 oz (75g) currants

3 oz (75g) pine nuts or chopped walnuts

1 teaspoon allspice

1½ teaspoons cinnamon

Salt and freshly ground black pepper to taste

1 tablespoon tomato purée

12 oz (350g) tinned or packed vine leaves

Juice of 2 lemons

Lemon wedges for garnish

Serves 4 to 6

Fry the onions in the oil in a heavy pan until soft and transparent. Add the rice and fry, stirring all the time, for 2 to 3 minutes. Add enough water to cover the rice and then stir in the currants, nuts and spices. Gently simmer until the rice is cooked (add a little more water if needed) and all the moisture is absorbed. Stir in the tomato purée and remove from the heat.

Meanwhile, put the tinned or packet vine leaves in a bowl and scald with boiling water. Leave them to soak and disentangle themselves. Transfer to a colander and rinse with cold water. (If you are using fresh leaves merely wash them and carefully cut out the central vein.) Place a teaspoon or more of the filling in the centre of each vine leaf. Roll the leaf over the filling, tucking in the sides as you go. Put some damaged leaves in the base of a heavy casserole dish and layer the stuffed leaves on top. If you have more than one layer, separate each layer with vine leaves. Then add enough water just to cover them, add the lemon juice and cover the casserole. Simmer for about 1 hour over a low heat. Alternatively, bake the dolmades in a low oven (300°F, 150°C, gas mark 2) for approximately 2 hours. Allow them to cool in the casserole. Drain and arrange them on a serving tray. Chill and serve with wedges of lemon for garnish.

SALADS

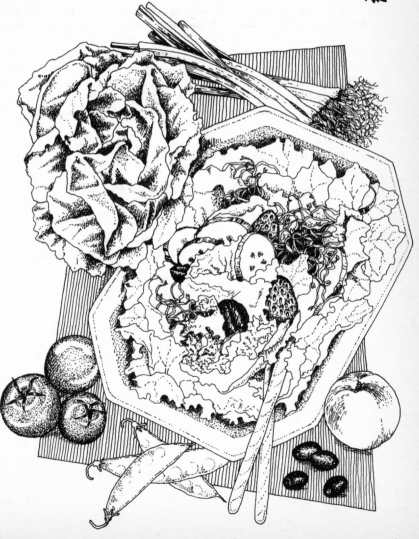

Salads have perhaps a greater versatility than any other dish and here I have given an unusual and exciting selection from countries around the world. All of them use ingredients available from any well-stocked greengrocer, supermarket or ethnic food store. They are easy to prepare and can add the flavour of faraway places to the simplest meal. Salads are good as side dishes, starters, appetizers, or light meals (for example, served with a dip and bread), and those containing grains or beans may be served as main dishes. Remember that when preparing a salad the taste, colour and texture of the salad vegetabless are most important, so buy the best ingredients you can find. Where possible buy them in season when they are both at their best and cheapest. Salads should please the eye, so care needs to be taken with their presentation.

To finish on a nutritional note, salads are an excellent source of many vitamins, minerals, small quantities of high-quality protein (the grain and bean salads are good protein dishes in their own right), and fibre. Most nutritionists recommend eating at least one large salad a day.

RICE AND LENTIL SALAD

This dish is popular in the Arab world. It is exceptionally nutritious and, like so many peasant dishes, very satisfying. Serve accompanied with a light green salad and a plate of dressed, sliced tomatoes.

8 oz (225g) large green or brown lentils, well picked over, washed, and soaked for 2 hours
1 medium onion, finely chopped
4 tablespoons olive oil
½ teaspoon ground cumin
Salt and freshly ground black pepper to taste
5 oz (150g) long grain brown rice

Garnish
1 medium onion, peeled and sliced vertically into crescent-shaped slices
1 clove garlic, crushed
4 tablespoons vegetable oil

Serves 4

Drain the lentils, cover with fresh water and bring to the boil. Reduce the heat and simmer for 15 minutes. Meanwhile, gently fry the chopped onion in the olive oil until it is soft and golden. Add the cooked onion and the seasonings to the lentils and cook brieflfy, then add the rice. Cover with additional water and bring back to the boil. Reduce the heat, place a lid on the pan and simmer for 40 minutes or until the rice and lentils are tender. Check during this period that there is enough water in the pan to prevent the rice drying out. Stir and check the seasoning, then spoon on to a serving dish and leave to cool.

For the garnish, fry the onion slices and garlic in very hot oil until they are browned and beginning to crisp. Serve the lentils and rice topped with the fried onion mixture.

PANZANELLA (TOMATO AND BREAD SALAD)

A fresh and filling salad from Tuscany, served as a substantial first course or a light meal.

5 oz (150g) coarse white
   bread, crusts removed
4 large ripe tomatoes
1 Spanish onion
½ cucumber
2 sticks celery
1 bunch fresh basil, chopped
   (if fresh basil is not
   available, parsley, mint or
   chives do equally well)
2 fl oz (50ml) olive oil
1 tablespoon wine vinegar
Salt and freshly ground black
   pepper to taste

Serves 4

Cut the bread into chunky pieces. Put in a salad bowl and sprinkle with cold water so that it is well moistened but not soggy. Add all the vegetables, sliced or cut into neat pieces and sprinkle with the chopped basil. Dress with the oil, vinegar, salt and pepper, toss well and leave for ½ to 1 hour so that the bread can absorb the dressing.

GRAPEFRUIT AND COCONUT SALAD

Serve this Thai salad as a starter or side dish. Where they are available pomelos may be substituted for the grapefruit.

4 oz (100g) desiccated coconut
1 teaspoon sugar
2 teaspoons soya sauce
2 tablespoons lemon juice
2 tablespoons water
2 teaspoons vegetable oil
1 clove garlic, crushed
2 tablespoons finely diced
   onion

Dry-roast the coconut in a frying pan (see page 18) until it just starts to brown. Turn it into a mixing bowl and stir in the sugar, soya sauce, lemon juice and water. Heat the oil in a small pan and stir-fry the garlic and onion until golden. Stir this mixture into the

2 large grapefruit, peeled and
segmented
Lettuce leaves to garnish

Serves 4

coconut. Arrange the grapefruit
segments on a few lettuce leaves on
individual plates. Pour some of the
coconut dressing over each and serve.

CHINESE SALAD WITH HOT DRESSING

*Shredded and sliced raw vegetables are covered with a stir-fried
dressing of olive oil, bamboo shoots, water chestnuts, ginger and
soya sauce.*

½ large lettuce, shredded
2 large carrots, peeled and cut
into matchsticks
½ medium cucumber, peeled,
deseeded and thinly sliced
6 spring onions, chopped
6 tablespoons olive oil
1 clove garlic, crushed
4 oz (100g) bamboo shoots,
cut into thin strips
3 water chestnuts, thinly sliced
1 tablespoon soya sauce
Salt and freshly ground black
pepper to taste
2 pieces preserved stem ginger,
finely chopped

Serves 4

Combine the lettuce, carrots and
cucumber in a salad bowl. Fry the
spring onions gently in the olive oil for
2 to 3 minutes. Add the garlic,
bamboo shoots and water chestnuts,
turn the heat up and stir-fry for 1 to 2
minutes. Remove from the heat, stir in
the soya sauce, salt and black pepper
to taste and ginger. Pour this mixture
over the salad and serve immediately.

BRUSSELS SPROUT AND APPLE SALAD

*For some reason many people do not like Brussels sprouts, perhaps
because as children they were forced to eat overcooked, soggy
specimens. However, they can be delicious both raw and cooked.
Buy sprouts that are a good green colour and not too large. Cook
them in a pan with a small amount of water (about 1in (2.5cm)) for
7 to 8 minutes, depending on their size. As soon as they are tender,
drain them and serve. Brussels sprouts are also surprisingly good in
salads. Try them in this recipe.*

2 tablespoons red wine
  vinegar
4 tablespoons olive oil
2 cloves garlic, crushed
1 teaspoon prepared mustard
1 tablespoon finely chopped
  fresh sage or parsley
Salt and freshly ground black
  pepper to taste
1 eating apple, cored and
  sliced
Juice of 1 lemon
4 spring onions, trimmed and
  chopped
12 oz (350g) Brussels sprouts,
  trimmed and finely
  shredded

Serves 4

Combine the vinegar, oil, garlic,
mustard, sage or parsley, and salt and
black pepper to taste. Mix well
together. Toss the apple slices in the
lemon juice. In a serving bowl
combine the spring onions, Brussels
sprouts, apple slices and dressing. Toss
well and serve.

COOKED SALAD

*Cooked salads are a great favourite in North Africa where they are
served as a side dish. They keep well and even improve the day after
preparation. Fresh coriander is essential to this salad.*

2 medium tomatoes, quartered
2 medium onions, coarsely
  diced
½ cucumber, sliced in half
  lengthwise, seeds scooped
  out, sliced
1 red or green pepper, seeded
  and chopped
4 tablespoons water
3 tablespoons olive oil
2 tablespoons lemon juice
2 cloves garlic, crushed
Salt and freshly ground black
  pepper to taste
2 tablespoons chopped fresh
  coriander leaves

Serves 4 to 6

Put the tomatoes, onions, cucumber,
red or green pepper and water into a
pan, simmer for 4 to 5 minutes and
then remove from the heat. Set the pan
aside. Beat together the oil, lemon
juice, garlic and salt and black pepper.
Strain any liquid from the pan then
pour the dressing on to the vegetables.
Add the chopped coriander and gently
mix. Transfer the salad to a serving
bowl and serve warm or at room
temperature.

INDONESIAN FRUIT SALAD

In this unusual salad fruits and vegetables are combined and served with a dressing made from chillies, vinegar, soya sauce and plenty of brown sugar. Any combination of fresh fruit or vegetables in season can be used. Serve the fruit salad on its own, as part of a larger meal alongside savoury dishes, or as the last course of a lunch.

2 Granny Smith apples, peeled and cut into pieces
2 oranges, peeled and segmented
1 grapefruit, peeled and segmented
½ fresh pineapple, peeled and cubed, or 1 small tin unsweetened pineapple, drained
1 or 2 firm mangoes, peeled and cut into pieces
½ cucumber, sliced
1 bunch radishes, washed, topped and tailed

Dressing
1 fresh or dried red chilli, seeds removed, finely chopped
1 tablespoon dark soya sauce
4 oz (100g) dark brown sugar
2 tablespoons white vinegar or lemon juice

Serves 4

Combine all the fruits and vegetables in a large bowl. Mix together all the dressing ingredients by hand or in a blender and then pour the dressing over the salad. Mix well and serve. The dressing can also be served in individual bowls into which the fruit and vegetables are dipped before eating.

GRILLED GREEN PEPPER SALAD

This is a recipe from Armenia. Serve cold with French bread or pitta bread.

4 medium green peppers
1 large clove garlic, thinly sliced

Wash and dry the peppers, then grill them under a moderate heat, turning 2 or 3 times, until the skins are lightly

2 tablespoons olive oil
1 tablespoon cider vinegar or
  wine vinegar
Salt to taste

Serves 4

charred. Rub or peel the skins off and cut off the stem end of each pepper. Remove the core and the seeds. Quarter each pepper lengthwise and arrange the quarters in a serving dish. Sprinkle over them the garlic, olive oil, vinegar and salt and set aside to chill.

RUSSIAN SALAD

This is a substantial but delicious salad simply made from readily available ingredients. Serve it with bread as a light meal on a cold day or as a side dish to a light stew or soup.

6 oz (175g) cooked beetroot,
  peeled and diced
6 oz (175g) cooked, but firm,
  potatoes, peeled and diced
2 medium eating apples, cored
  and diced
2 medium carrots, peeled and
  diced
1 tablespoon prepared
  mustard
4 tablespoons vegetable oil
Salt to taste

Serves 4

Combine the beetroot, potatoes, apples and carrots. Stir the mustard into the oil to form a paste. Stir this into the vegetables and set aside for 1 hour before serving.

TABBOULEH

Tabbouleh is a Middle Eastern salad made with burghul (bulgar) wheat, lots of fresh parsley, mint and lemon juice. There is no specific recipe and the way the salad is prepared is very much up to individual taste.

The recipe given here is a guide and you should alter the amounts to suit your own preferences. Serve as a starter, side salad or main dish salad. It's also very good as a filling in pitta bread with falafel (see page 145).

8 oz (225g) fine bulgar wheat
8 oz (225g) onion and/or
  spring onion, finely
  chopped
2 bunches fresh parsley,
  chopped
4 tablespoons chopped fresh
  mint, or 1 tablespoon
  crushed dried mint
3 medium tomatoes, finely
  chopped
4 fl oz (100ml) lemon juice
4 fl oz (100ml) olive oil
1 teaspoon allspice (optional)
Salt and freshly ground black
  pepper to taste
Wedges of lemon for garnish

Serves 4 to 6

Cover the bulgar wheat with plenty of very hot water and leave for 15 minutes until swollen. Drain in a colander and squeeze out any excess water by gently pressing the wheat with your hand. Put the wheat into a large serving bowl and gently stir in all the remaining ingredients except the lemon wedges. Taste, and adjust the seasoning if necessary. Garnish with lemon wedges and serve.

TABBOULEH-FILLED MUSHROOMS

½ quantity of tabbouleh
  (recipe above)
6 very large mushroom caps,
  stalks removed
Mint or parsley sprigs to
  garnish

Serves 6

Half-fill a large saucepan with water and bring to the boil. Put the mushrooms into the water and return to the boil. Cook gently, covered, for 3 minutes then drain off the water and set the mushrooms aside to cool. Fill the caps with the tabbouleh, garnish with the mint or parsley sprigs and serve.

CHERRY AND WALNUT SALAD

This unusual savoury fruit salad may be served as a starter or a side dish.

2 oz (50g) walnuts, chopped
1 medium orange

Wash, halve and stone the cherries, reserving a few whole ones with stalks

½ Cos lettuce, separated into leaves
Vinaigrette dressing to taste (see page 27)
12 oz (350g) black cherries

Serves 4

for garnish. Peel the orange, remove all pith and slice thinly with a sharp knife. Arrange the lettuce leaves round the edges of a shallow serving dish and place the orange slices on top. Toss the cherries in a little vinaigrette dressing, add the walnuts and pile up in the centre of the dish. Garnish with the reserved whole cherries.

SWEET AND SOUR VEGETABLE AND BEANCURD SALAD

Cubes of beancurd are marinated in a sweet and sour dressing and then mixed with raw, chopped vegetables in this Western adaptation of a Southeast Asian salad.

2 tablespoons sesame oil
3 tablespoons soya sauce
3 tablespoons cider vinegar
1 tablespoon water
1 teaspoon clear honey
1 clove garlic, crushed
2 blocks (total weight 12 oz/ 350g) beancurd, cut into 1 in (2.5cm) cubes
2 stalks celery, finely chopped
2 oz (50g) mushrooms, washed and sliced
4 oz (100g) Chinese or white cabbage, finely shredded

Serves 4 to 6

Combine the oil, soya sauce, vinegar, water, honey and garlic and mix well together. Put two-thirds of this mixture into a large shallow bowl or container and add the beancurd cubes. Leave them to marinate in the refrigerator for 1 hour.

Transfer the beancurd and marinade to a serving bowl and gently stir in the celery, mushrooms and cabbage. Add the remaining dressing, carefully toss the salad and serve.

MIDDLE EASTERN SALAD

Salads of lettuce, cucumber, tomatoes and onion are popular everywhere in the Middle East. The quantity of each ingredient and the way they are combined depends on personal choice and local tradition. Below is one suggested combination.

1 small lettuce, shredded by hand
1 cucumber, thinly sliced
2 tomatoes, quartered
1 bunch spring onions, chopped
1 medium mild onion, diced
1 bunch parsley, finely chopped
2 tablespoons chopped fresh mint or 1 teaspoon dried mint

Dressing
1 clove garlic, peeled, halved if large
2 fl oz (50ml) olive oil or other vegetable oil
3 tablespoons lemon juice
Salt and freshly ground black pepper to taste

Serves 4

Rub the inside of a large bowl with the clove of garlic. Combine the remaining ingredients for the dressing and add the clove of garlic, crushed. Mix well. Put the vegetables and herbs into the bowl, mix well, toss with the dressing and serve.

CHILLED AUBERGINE SALAD

Cooked, cold aubergines make a good and unusual salad ingredient. Try them in a rice or bean salad or as a main ingredient, as in this recipe.

2 medium aubergines, cut into ¾ in (2cm) cubes
6 oz (175g) shallots, finely chopped
6 tablespoons olive oil
1 clove garlic, crushed
Finely grated rind of ½ orange
6 tablespoons white wine
Salt and freshly ground black pepper to taste
1 orange, peeled, segmented and chopped, for garnish

Serves 4

Put the cubed aubergines into a colander and sprinkle generously with salt. Leave to drain for 30 minutes. Pat dry with absorbent paper. Fry the chopped shallots gently in 2 tablespoons of the olive oil for 3 minutes. Add the garlic and fry gently for a further minute. Add the remaining oil and then add the aubergine cubes to the pan; fry gently for 3 to 4 minutes. Add the orange rind, white wine and salt and black pepper to taste. Simmer gently until

the aubergine is just tender (about 5
minutes). Allow to cool and then chill.
Spoon on to 4 small serving plates and
garnish with the chopped orange
segments.

FRENCH BEAN AND BLACK OLIVE SALAD

*Young French beans at their best should be crisp and snap easily
when broken in two. They need only a minimum of cooking and the
cooked beans should still have some crunch. A variation on this
salad which makes it more substantial is given below.*

1 lb (450g) young French
  beans, topped only
4 tablespoons olive oil
2 tablespoons lemon juice
Salt and freshly ground black
  pepper to taste
2 oz (50g) black olives (stone
  and chop 4 or 5 olives, leave
  the rest whole)

Serves 4

Put the beans in a large pan of salted
boiling water and cook for 10 minutes
or less. Drain them, rinse immediately
under cold running water, drain again
and then put them into a salad bowl.
Add the oil, lemon juice, black pepper
and whole olives. Toss well and chill
slightly before serving garnished with
the chopped olives.

Variation
For an unusual and nutritious
variation add 6 oz (175g) beancurd,
pressed (see page 22) and then fried in
a little oil.

WHITE CABBAGE AND FRUIT SALAD

*This is a crunchy winter salad that makes a good alternative to the
more familiar Waldorf salad.*

½ medium white cabbage,
  finely shredded
Vinaigrette dressing to taste
  (see page 27)

Put the shredded cabbage into a salad
bowl and stir in sufficient dressing just
to moisten it. Add the other
ingredients, mix well and serve.

4 sticks celery, cut into thin,
   matchstick-length strips
2 eating apples, cored and
   chopped
4 oz (100g) grapes, halved and
   seeded
2 oz (50g) walnuts, chopped
1 tablespoon chopped fresh
   chives (optional)
Salt and freshly ground black
   pepper to taste

Serves 4

SYRIAN BULGAR SALAD

*Bulgar wheat salads are usually made with parsley and lemon juice
but this version uses spices and herbs. It is flavoursome and a good
accompaniment to cooked vegetables or on its own as a main-course
lunch dish.*

12 oz (350g) fine bulgar wheat
1 large onion, finely diced
2 fl oz (50ml) olive oil
2 oz (50g) tomato purée
2 oz (50g) pine nuts or
   chopped walnuts, dry-
   roasted (see page 18)
1 tablespoon dried oregano
2 tablespoons chopped fresh
   parsley
1 teaspoon ground coriander
1 teaspoon ground cumin
½ teaspoon ground allspice
Salt, freshly ground black
   pepper and cayenne pepper
   to taste

Serves 6

Cover the bulgar wheat with very hot
water and leave to soak for 15 minutes
or until swollen. Drain well. Sauté the
onion in a little of the oil until just
soft and transparent. Combine the
onion and remaining ingredients with
the bulgar wheat and mix well
together. Put in the refrigerator for 2
to 3 hours or longer to allow the
flavours to blend, then serve.

CHINESE BROWN RICE SALAD

A substantial and nutritious salad with a well-flavoured dressing.

8 oz (225g) brown rice,
  cooked and drained
11 oz (300g) tinned bamboo
  shoots, drained and sliced
2 oz (50g) button mushrooms,
  wiped and sliced
4 oz (100g) beansprouts,
  rinsed and drained
1 bunch spring onions,
  trimmed and chopped
4 oz (100g) cooked beans (red
  beans, chickpeas or broad
  beans etc.) or sweetcorn
4 tablespoons medium sherry
1½ tablespoons natural soya
  sauce
2 tablespoons wine vinegar
3 tablespoons vegetable oil
  (sesame oil is good with this
  recipe)

Serves 4

Combine the rice, bamboo shoots, mushrooms, beansprouts, spring onions and beans or sweetcorn in a salad bowl. Mix together the sherry, soya sauce, vinegar and oil and pour this dressing over the rice salad. Toss well and serve.

CELERIAC, BEANSPROUT AND MANGETOUT SALAD

Celeriac looks like a small swede with a knobbly skin. It tends to be neglected in the UK but it has a fine flavour and makes a good salad ingredient. The French often serve it as a crudité. In this winter salad celeriac is combined with beansprouts and mangetout peas. Buy only very young mangetout with flat pods.

1 medium head celeriac
Juice of 1 lemon
4 oz (100g) small mangetout,
  washed and drained
4 oz (100g) fresh beansprouts,
  washed and drained

Peel the celeriac and grate or shred it coarsely; mix with the lemon juice immediately to prevent it discolouring. Mix the celeriac, mangetout and beansprouts together in a salad bowl. For the dressing, mix together the

Dressing
5 tablespoons olive oil
Juice of ½ lemon
Pinch of caster sugar
Salt and freshly ground black
  pepper to taste
1 clove garlic, crushed
2 tablespoons chopped fresh
  parsley

Serves 4 to 6

olive oil, lemon juice, sugar, salt and black pepper to taste, garlic and parsley. Spoon the dressing over the vegetables and toss together.

HERB AND LEMON POTATO SALAD

2 lb (900g) potatoes
1 medium onion, finely diced
3 tablespoons finely chopped
  fresh parsley
1 tablespoon finely chopped
  fresh mint or 1 teaspoon
  dried mint
2 cloves garlic, crushed
Juice of 1 medium lemon
3 tablespoons olive oil
Salt and freshly ground black
  pepper to taste

Serves 6

Scrub the potatoes and boil them in their jackets in plenty of salted water until they are just tender. Do not overcook. Drain them, and as soon as they are cool enough, peel off the skins. Cut the potatoes into small cubes and combine with the onion, parsley and mint. Mix the garlic, lemon juice, olive oil and seasoning and pour it over the salad. Toss well and serve.

Variation:
Potato and Green Bean Salad
Follow the recipe above but replace the onion by 8 oz (225g) green beans. Top and tail them, cut into 2 in (5cm) lengths and cook in a little salted water until they are almost tender but still crisp. Drain, cool and combine with the potatoes.

THREE GREENS SALAD

Three varieties of green vegetables are parcooked and, while still warm, tossed in vinaigrette dressing. The dressing is absorbed as the salad cools.

1 small cauliflower, cut into florets
2 courgettes, sliced into rounds
6 oz (175g) French beans, left whole
Vinaigrette dressing (see page 27)

Serves 4

Bring a little salted water to the boil in a saucepan. Add the cauliflower, cover and simmer for 3 minutes. Add the courgettes and French beans and simmer for a further 5 minutes. Do not overcook as they are best a little crunchy. Remove the pan from the heat, drain the vegetables and briefly rinse them under the cold tap. Drain them again and transfer them to a salad bowl. Toss in a little vinaigrette dressing and leave to cool to room temperature before serving.

VEGETABLES

Good-quality vegetables simply cooked and served on their own are quite delicious enough to grace our tables, but vegetables can also provide the basis for tasty and interesting main-course dishes. A collection of simple and versatile recipes for such dishes is given here. The recipes do not always have to be followed exactly since ingredients and amounts can be changed to suit both what is seasonably available and the cook's imagination.

Vegetables are an important source of vitamins, particularly vitamin C, minerals, dietary fibre and carbohydrate. Green vegetables in addition contain small amounts of high-quality protein. The roots, the part we eat, of vegetables such as potatoes, parsnips, swedes and turnips are where energy is stored in the plant, and they are a good source of starches and natural sugars.

Buy pesticide-free, organically grown vegetables if you can find a supply of them. Always wash vegetables, wherever they come from, and if necessary give them a good scrub. Peel them if you suspect the skin may contain pesticides or other chemicals; otherwise leave unpeeled, since many nutrients are found in the skin or just beneath. If the vegetables are to be served on their own, cook as briefly as possible in the minimum of water so that they retain their colour and texture.

Vegetables for both cooking and salads are best bought in season, when they are at their tastiest and cheapest. This will probably be because they have been grown locally, or at least nationally, and will be both fresh and plentiful. Imported vegetables may be added for variety and extra interest.

MARROW AND TOMATOES WITH CRUNCHY TOPPING

A good autumn dish when marrow and other squash plants (which may be substituted) are both good quality and cheap.

3 oz (75g) vegetable margarine
1 small clove garlic, crushed
1 large onion, finely chopped
1½ lb (675g) marrow, diced
4 tomatoes, skinned, seeded and coarsely chopped (see page 30)
Good pinch of cayenne pepper
Salt

Preheat the oven to 400°F (200°C, gas mark 6).

Lightly grease a gratin dish. Heat the margarine in a frying pan, add the garlic and onion and sauté until transparent but not brown. Stir in the marrow, tomatoes, cayenne pepper and salt to taste. Cover and cook over

2 oz (50g) fresh brown
   breadcrumbs
2 tablespoons olive oil

Serves 4

a low heat for about 10 minutes or
until the marrow is tender but not too
soft. Shake the pan occasionally to
prevent the vegetables from sticking.
Spoon the mixture into the gratin
dish. Fry the breadcrumbs in the olive
oil until they are crisp and the oil is
absorbed. Sprinkle over the vegetables
and place in the preheated oven for
about 10 minutes until the top is
brown and crisp. Serve immediately.

POTATO GNOCCHI

Serve these potato dumplings with a hot horseradish sauce, see next recipe.

1½ lbs (675g) potatoes
6 oz (175g) cornflour
Salt and freshly ground black
   pepper to taste
8 fl oz (225ml) water

Serves 4

Boil the potatoes in their jackets.
Leave to cool for half an hour, then
peel and mash them. Mix the
cornflour into the potatoes and season
to taste with salt and pepper. Bring the
water to the boil, pour it over the
mixture and mix well with a whisk.
Using a dessertspoon, form little
dumplings and lower them gently into
a large saucepan of boiling, salted
water. Simmer for about 10 minutes or
until the gnocchi float to the surface
of the pan. Lift out gently and serve
with horseradish sauce.

HORSERADISH SAUCE

2 oz (50g) vegetable margarine
2 oz (50g) plain flour
1 teaspoon English mustard
   powder

Melt the margarine in a saucepan, add
the flour and mustard powder and
cook for 2 to 3 minutes, stirring all

1 pint (550ml) vegetable stock
(see page 26)
1 teaspoon sugar
4 tablespoons wine vinegar or
cider vinegar
3 oz (75g) grated horseradish
1 tablespoon chopped fresh
parsley

the time. Add the stock and cook for
10 minutes, stirring from time to time.
Stir in the sugar and vinegar, take off
the heat and add the grated
horseradish and the parsley.

STUFFED CHINESE MUSHROOMS WITH SHERRY SAUCE

*Black dehydrated Chinese mushrooms have large caps and are perfect
for stuffing. This recipe also requires bamboo shoots. Buy a very
small tin and store unused shoots under clear water. Use them within
three or four days. The stuffed mushrooms are served garnished with
fresh coriander leaves, sometimes known as Chinese parsley. They
give the dish a characteristic flavour but, if unavailable, parsley may
be substituted.*

8 dehydrated Chinese black
mushrooms
5 oz (150g) brown or white
rice, parcooked
1 tablespoon finely chopped
bamboo shoots
1 spring onion, chopped
2 tablespoons soya sauce
2 tablespoons medium-sweet
sherry
2 tablespoons peanut or other
vegetable oil
2 tablespoons vegetable stock
or water
1 teaspoon cornflour
¼ teaspoon salt

Garnish
Coriander leaves, finely
chopped

Serves 4

Cover the mushrooms in warm water
and leave to soak for 30 minutes.
Drain well and discard the hard,
inedible stalks. Combine the rice,
bamboo shoots, spring onion, half the
soya sauce and half the sherry. Stir this
mixture into a paste and fill the
mushroom caps with it. Put the caps
in a steamer (or between 2 plates
standing on a bowl in a pan with
water in the bottom) and steam for 20
minutes. Just before they are ready,
put the oil, vegetable stock or water,
cornflour, salt and remaining soya
sauce and sherry in a small pan and
heat, stirring, until just boiling. Serve
the mushrooms with the hot sauce
poured over and garnished with
coriander leaves.

GRILLED SWEET POTATOES

Sweet potatoes are delicious and filling. They taste best cooked in a simple and straightforward manner, such as the one below. Serve with vegetables. Sweet potatoes may also be used as an interesting substitute for potatoes in other recipes.

8 small or 4 medium sweet
   potatoes
2 tablespoons olive oil

Serves 4

Put the sweet potatoes in a pan of salted water and bring to the boil. Cover, reduce heat and simmer for 10 to 15 minutes (depending on size). Drain, split the potatoes in half. Criss-cross the open faces with a sharp knife, brush with the oil and grill, open side up, until browned and tender.

ASPARAGUS IN WALNUT AND TARRAGON SAUCE

Asparagus is one of the delights of the culinary year, and although it may be quite expensive you do not have to serve a special main dish to accompany it. Nor does it have to be just a starter to a multi-course meal. For a simple feast that won't cost you a fortune serve freshly cooked asparagus with walnut and tarragon sauce, minted new potatoes and a salad of crisp lettuce leaves. Cooked asparagus is also good served cold with an oil and vinegar or other dressing, and in flans, salads and even sandwiches.

1½ lb (675g) asparagus
½ oz (15g) vegetable
   margarine
½ oz (15g) plain flour
¼ pint (150ml) soya milk
Salt and freshly ground black
   pepper to taste
1 tablespoon finely chopped
   fresh tarragon
½ oz (15g) walnuts, chopped
3 tablespoons asparagus
   cooking water

Serves 4

Tie the asparagus into individual serving-sized bundles, stand them, heads up, in a saucepan and cook them in gently boiling salted water for 5 to 15 minutes, depending on the thickness of the stems. The heads themselves should steam above the level of the water. Take good care not to overcook.

Meanwhile melt the margarine in a saucepan, stir in the flour and cook for less than a minute. Slowly pour in the soya milk, stirring constantly, and then add salt and black pepper to taste. Bring to the boil, reduce the heat and simmer for a few minutes. Stir in the tarragon, walnuts and asparagus water. Simmer for a further 2 minutes. Drain the asparagus and serve hot with the sauce.

Note Other fresh herbs as available may be used for the sauce.

VALENCIAN BAKED VEGETABLES AND RICE

This simple dish from Valencia in Spain is easy to prepare and very tasty. Fortunately this type of peasant recipe is beginning to find favour with Spanish chefs, and tourists are now more likely to taste real Spanish food as opposed to the bland international dishes 'traditionally' served in holiday hotels.

2 tablespoons olive oil
1 large onion, finely chopped
4 cloves garlic, crushed
2 medium carrots, finely chopped
6 to 8 oz (175 to 225g) fresh tomatoes, chopped, or tinned tomatoes, drained weight, chopped
8 oz (225g) rice
½ teaspoon turmeric
¼ teaspoon cayenne pepper
Salt and freshly ground black pepper to taste
6 oz (175g) tinned chickpeas (optional)

Serves 4 to 6

Preheat the oven to 375°F (190°,gas mark 5).

Use a little of the oil to grease an 8×8in (20×20cm) oven-to-table baking dish. Heat the remaining oil in a large pan and add the onion and garlic. Stir and cook over a moderate heat until the onions soften. Add the carrots, then after a few minutes add the tomatoes, reduce the heat to low and cook, stirring occasionally, for 10 minutes. Leave the lid off the pan. Add the rice, turmeric, cayenne pepper, salt and black pepper and stir over the heat for 2 or 3 minutes. Stir in the drained chickpeas, if using and boiling water to cover. Transfer the contents of the pan to the baking dish and bake in the preheated oven for 20 to 25 minutes or until the rice is tender and most of the liquid is absorbed.

VEGETABLE BHAJIS

Bhajis are spicy Indian side dishes made with one or two vegetables, or occasionally with more. They are usually eaten with rice, puris or chapattis and dal. Bhajis are cooked in a minimum of water and where possible the vegetables' own moisture is used as the cooking medium. Boiling vegetables is considered by the Indian cook to kill the goodness in them and this method of cooking is not used in Indian cuisine. The less water and the slower the cooking time, the better the taste, is a good general rule for cooks new to Indian food.

Here is a selection of three vegetable bhaji dishes. Each serves four people as a side dish and may be prepared individually to accompany a main curry dish. Alternatively prepare two or three of them and serve with chapattis, rice and salad for a simple Indian meal.

AUBERGINE BHAJI

3 tablespoons vegetable oil
4 cloves garlic, crushed
1 teaspoon turmeric powder
1 teaspoon cumin seeds
1 to 2 green chillies, finely chopped
1 in (2.5cm) piece ginger root, grated
1 lb (450g) aubergines, cut into ¾ ini (2cm) cubes, salted, pressed for 30 minutes, rinsed and drained
1 teaspoon garam masala, or to taste

Serves 4

Heat the oil in a heavy saucepan or casserole and sauté the garlic until golden. Stir in the turmeric and cumin seeds and mix well, then add the chilli, ginger and aubergine and stir. Cover and cook over a very low heat for 20 minutes. Remove the lid from the pan and cook uncovered until most of the moisture has evaporated and the aubergine is tender. Sprinkle over the garam masala and heat through, then serve.

Note Slicing and salting aubergines before use draws off their slightly bitter juices and it also reduces the amount of oil they absorb.

CAULIFLOWER BHAJI

3 tablespoons vegetable oil
1 medium potato, peeled and
  finely diced
1 teaspoon turmeric
½ teaspoon cumin seeds
1 in (2.5cm) piece ginger root,
  very thinly sliced
½ teaspoon chilli powder
  (optional)
1 medium cauliflower, cut into
  even-sized florets
Salt and freshly ground black
  pepper to taste

Serves 4

In a heavy saucepan or casserole heat the oil and add the potato, turmeric, cumin seeds, ginger and chilli powder, if using. Stir-fry for 2 minutes. Add the cauliflower and sauté over a low heat for 5 minutes, then add salt to taste. Cover the pan and cook over a gentle heat until the cauliflower is tender (10 to 15 minutes). Serve sprinkled with freshly ground black pepper.

Variation: Okra Bhaji
To make Bhindi Bhaji (okra), replace the cauliflower with 1 lb (450g) young okra pods. If the pods are young and tender use them whole; otherwise they will have to be sliced.

SPINACH BHAJI

1½ lb (675g) fresh spinach or
  10 oz (275g) frozen spinach,
  defrosted
2 tablespoons vegetable oil
1 medium onion, thinly sliced
2 cloves garlic, crushed
1 teaspoon cumin seeds
1 teaspoon turmeric powder
1 to 2 dried red chillies,
  crushed (use less or none at
  all if you dislike hot food)
1 in (2.5cm) piece ginger root,
  grated
Salt to taste

Serves 4

Pick over the spinach, remove any bad leaves and cut off thick stalks. Coarsely chop the leaves if they are big; wash well and drain. Ignore this stage if using frozen spinach. Heat the oil in a large heavy saucepan or casserole with a lid and fry the onion and garlic, stirring constantly, until light brown. Stir in the cumin seeds and turmeric and then the chilli and ginger. Sauté for 1 minute. Add the spinach and cook, covered, over a low-to-moderate heat for 8 to 10 minutes or until the spinach is wilted. Add salt to taste and cook, uncovered, until nearly all the liquid has gone. Cover

the pot and cook for a further 5
minutes over a gentle heat. Serve.

FRESH TOMATO TART

*This recipe provides a convenient and tasty way of using up soft,
overripe tomatoes.*

6 oz (175g) wholewheat
shortcrust pastry (see page
26)
1 tablespoon olive oil
1½ lb (675g) tomatoes,
chopped
1 large clove garlic, peeled and
crushed
Salt and freshly ground black
pepper to taste
3 tablespoons tomato purée
½ teaspoon grated orange
rind
1 teaspoon chopped fresh
mint
½ teaspoon brown sugar

Serves 4 to 6

Preheat the oven to 375°F (190°C, gas
mark 5).

Roll out the pastry thinly and use to
line an 8 in (20cm) loose-bottomed
flan tin. Press up the edges well and
pinch neatly. Line with greaseproof
paper, fill with baking beans and bake
blind for 10 minutes. Meanwhile
prepare the filling. Heat the oil in a
large shallow pan. Add the tomatoes,
garlic, salt and black pepper, and cook
gently for 5 minutes. Add the tomato
purée, orange rind, mint and sugar.
Cook gently for 10 to 15 minutes until
the sauce is thick and richly coloured.
Spread the tomato mixture evenly in
the par-baked pastry case and return
to the oven for 30 minutes. Serve
warm, cut into wedges.

AUBERGINES AND TOMATOES COOKED
WITH SOYA SAUCE

Serve with boiled rice or as an accompaniment to other dishes.

2 medium aubergines, thickly
sliced, each slice cut in half
to form semi-circles
2 tablespoons vegetable oil
1 medium onion, sliced

Sprinkle the aubergine slices liberally
with salt and leave them in a colander
to stand for 30 minutes. Rinse them
under cold water and dry them on
absorbent kitchen paper. Heat the oil

2 cloves garlic, crushed
8 oz (225g) ripe tomatoes,
skinned and chopped (see
page 30), or tinned tomatoes,
drained and chopped
½ teaspoon chilli powder
2 tablespoons dark soya sauce
2 teaspoons dark brown sugar
Salt and freshly ground black
pepper to taste

Serves 4

in a saucepan over a moderate heat
and sauté the onion and garlic until
the onion is softened. Add the
aubergines and sauté for 2 to 3
minutes. Add the remaining
ingredients and mix well. Cover the
pan and simmer for 10 minutes,
stirring occasionally. Adjust the
seasoning and serve.

MIXED VEGETABLES IN COCONUT MILK

This dish, called in Indonesian sayur lodeh, *is thin and soupy. It is
served with boiled rice, which is moistened with liquid from the*
sayur *before being eaten. As with other recipes of this type, any
seasonal vegetables can be used. I have given a suggested
combination which illustrates the order in which vegetables with
different cooking times should be added to the pot.*

2 tablespoons vegetable oil
1 small onion, finely diced
2 cloves garlic, crushed
1 red chilli, finely chopped, or
  ½ teaspoon chilli powder
1 teaspoon grated lemon rind
10 fl oz (275ml) vegetable
  stock (see page 26) or water
¾ pint (450ml) coconut milk
4 oz (100g) French beans cut
  into 1 in (2.5cm) lengths
4 oz (100g) aubergines, cubed,
  salted, pressed for 30
  minutes, rinsed and drained
4 oz (100g) cabbage, coarsely
  shredded
Salt to taste

Serves 4

Heat the oil in a heavy saucepan, add
the onion and garlic and sauté until
the onion is softened. Add the chilli
and lemon rind, stir and cook for 2 to
3 minutes. Add the stock or water and
the coconut milk and bring to a low
boil, stirring. Put in the French beans
and simmer for 3 minutes. Add the
aubergines and simmer for another 3
minutes. Finally, add the cabbage and
the salt and simmer until all the
vegetables are just tender (another 5
minutes approximately). Serve.

CUMIN AND OLIVE FRIED POTATOES

An unusual way to serve the common but highly versatile potato. This dish is excellent with bread as a filling, simple meal or as a side dish to grains or beans; or serve it with a mixed salad for a light lunch.

1½ lb (675g) potatoes, peeled
3 tablespoons olive oil
1 small onion, finely chopped
2 cloves garlic, crushed
1 teaspoon ground cumin
4 oz (100g) black olives, stoned
Salt and freshly ground black pepper to taste

Serves 4

Boil the potatoes until almost tender but still firm. Drain them and cool under running cold water, then cut into 1 in (2.5cm) cubes and pat dry. Heat the oil in a frying pan and lightly sauté the onion and garlic. Add the potatoes, cumin and olives and stir-fry over a gentle heat until the potatoes are tender and the olives very hot. Season to taste and serve.

WINTER VEGETABLE HOTPOT

This is a warm and filling winter dish, quick to prepare.

1 lb (450g) swedes, peeled and thickly sliced
1 small turnip, scrubbed and thinly sliced
2 medium carrots, scrubbed and thinly sliced
4 oz (100g) mushrooms, left whole
1 large onion, sliced
8 oz (225g) tomatoes, skinned and chopped (see page 30)
1 tablespoon miso
¼ teaspoon curry powder
1 pint (550ml) boiling vegetable stock (see page 26) or water

Serves 6

Preheat the oven to 350°F (180°C, gas mark 4).

Place all the ingredients in a casserole dish in alternate layers. Stir the miso and curry powder into the boiling stock or water and pour this over the vegetables. Cover and bake for 1½ hours in the preheated oven.

BAKED ROOT VEGETABLES

A simple, very economical but surprisingly tasty dish.

2 medium onions, sliced
1oz (25g) vegetable margarine
8 oz (225g) turnips, thinly
  sliced
8 oz (225g) parsnips, thinly
  sliced
1 lb (450g) carrots, thinly
  sliced
2 cloves garlic, crushed
3 tablespoons finely chopped
  fresh parsley
¾ pint (450ml) vegetable
  stock (see page 26) or water
1 tablespoon coarse mustard
Salt and freshly ground black
  pepper to taste

Serves 6

Preheat the oven to 350°F (180°C, gas mark 4).

In an oven- and flameproof dish, sauté the onions in the margarine until softened. Add the turnips, parsnips and carrots, stir well and sauté a further minute. Add the garlic, parsley, stock or water, and mustard and bring to a slow boil. Season to taste with salt and black pepper. Cover and bake in the preheated oven for 1 hour or until the vegetables are just tender.

SOUR VEGETABLES

This Indonesian dish consists of parboiled vegetables in a thin sauce and is similar to a soup. It is served with rice which complements it perfectly. The sour taste comes from the addition of tamarind water, but lemon juice can be substituted if this is unavailable.

1 small onion, finely diced
2 cloves garlic, crushed
1 small red or green chilli,
  finely chopped, or ½
  teaspoon chilli powder
5 almonds, crushed
¾ pint (450ml) water or
  vegetable stock (see page
  26)
8 oz (225g) raw peanuts
2 bay leaves
4 oz (100g) green or French
  beans, cut into 1 in (2.5cm)
  lengths

Put the onion, garlic, chilli, almonds and half the water or stock into a blender and blend the mixture to a thin paste. Transfer the paste to a small pan, bring to the boil and simmer for 5 minutes. Meanwhile, put the peanuts, bay leaves and remaining water or stock in another pan and boil for 5 minutes. Combine the contents of the two pans and add the green or French beans. Simmer for 3 to 4 minutes, then add the aubergines and

1 medium aubergine, cubed,
  salted, pressed for 30
  minutes, washed and
  drained
2 medium courgettes, sliced
4 cabbage leaves, coarsely
  chopped
4 tablespoons tamarind water
  or lemon juice
Salt to taste

Serves 4

courgettes. Simmer for 5 minutes and add the cabbage leaves, tamarind water or lemon juice, and salt. Simmer for a further 5 minutes or until all the vegetables are just tender, then serve.

VEGETABLE CURRY

A green and golden curry with a subtle flavour. Serve with wholemeal chapattis.

1 lb (450g) cauliflower
1 lb (450g) potatoes, diced
8 oz (225g) frozen peas
2 oz (50g) vegetable margarine
4 teaspoons mild curry paste
1 oz (25g) wholemeal flour
2 oz (50g) roasted peanuts
¾ pint (450ml) vegetable
  stock (made with 1
  vegetable stock cube)

Serves 4

Divide the cauliflower into florets. Boil the cauliflower and diced potatoes for several minutes until almost tender then add the peas. Melt the margarine in a large pan and stir in the curry paste. Cook over a low heat, stirring occasionally, for 5 to 6 minutes. Stir in the flour, add the peanuts and the vegetable stock and simmer until the sauce is smooth and thickened, stirring occasionally. Add the drained, cooked vegetables and toss them in the sauce, coating well. Simmer gently for 8 to 10 minutes. Serve at once.

RATATOUILLE

When properly cooked, ratatouille is one of the most delicious of all vegetable dishes. The vegetables should be just tender, brightly coloured and sitting in a thick sauce. The use of at least two frying pans simplifies its preparation. It is essential to use olive oil, small, firm aubergines and courgettes, and to rid the tomatoes of excess liquid. Ratatouille keeps well in the refrigerator and you may like to make twice this quantity and store half of it.

12 oz (350g) small aubergines, cut into ½ in (1.25cm) slices
12 oz (350g) small courgettes, cut into ½ in (1.25cm) slices
2 medium onions, sliced
¼ pint (150ml) olive oil
2 medium red or green peppers, stem and seeds removed, sliced
2 to 3 cloves of garlic, finely sliced
1 lb (450g) ripe tomatoes, skinned, seeds and excess liquid squeezed out and roughly chopped (see page 30)
a sprig of thyme
Salt and freshly ground black pepper to taste
1 tablespoon chopped fresh parsley
10 basil leaves (optional)

Serves 4

Unless the aubergines and courgettes are very young and firm, salt them and leave them to stand for an hour in a colander to drain the juices out. Gently pat the slices dry on absorbent kitchen paper.

Cook the onions in 2 tablespoons of the oil over a medium heat for 5 minutes until they begin to soften. Reduce the heat, add the peppers and the garlic and cook gently for a further 15 minutes, or until the vegetables are just tender. Set aside. Place 2 tablespoons of the oil in a saucepan over a brisk heat, add the tomatoes and quickly (2 to 3 minutes) reduce them to a thick pulp. Add the thyme, season with salt and pepper and add to the onions and peppers. Brown the courgette slices for 6 to 8 minutes in another 2 tablespoons of the oil in a frying pan over brisk heat, drain and set aside. Brown the aubergine slices in a similar manner but in twice as much oil, drain and add these to the courgettes.

Combine all the cooked vegetables and the parsley in a casserole set on an extremely low heat. Stir gently together and check the seasoning. The ratatouille is now ready to serve. It may be served warm, but it is at its best cold. If you have fresh basil available chop it up and stir it in just before serving.

VEGETABLE FRITTERS

Serve these fritters with potatoes and a green vegetable. Skordhalia (see page 53), a garlic dip, is good to dunk the fritters into.

Oil for shallow-frying
8 oz (225g) courgettes, thickly sliced
2 carrots, thickly sliced
½ cauliflower, broken into small florets
8 oz (225g) button mushrooms
Lemon wedges to garnish

Batter
4 oz (100g) chickpea flour
½ teaspoon salt
½ teaspoon chilli sauce
12 fl oz (325ml) cold water

Serves 4

To make the batter, mix the chickpea flour, salt and chilli sauce with the water until the mixture is completely smooth and thick. Heat the oil in a large frying pan, dip the vegetable pieces in the batter and fry in the shallow oil, a few pieces at a time, until both sides are golden. Remove, drain on kitchen paper, and keep warm while the rest of the vegetables are being fried. Serve the fritters, garnished with lemon wedges and accompanied by Skordhalia if you wish.

SPICED CHICKPEA AND POTATO DISH

A spicy, lemon-flavoured vegetable dish with a Middle Eastern flavour. Simple and quick to prepare if you have tinned chickpeas available. Serve with bread or a cooked grain such as rice or couscous.

2 tablespoons vegetable oil
2 medium onions, diced
½ teaspoon cumin powder
½ teaspoon coriander powder
¼ teaspoon ground ginger
1 teaspoon turmeric
¼ teaspoon chilli powder
Juice of 1 lemon
1 lb 12 oz (800g) tinned chickpeas, drained
2 medium tomatoes, quartered
3 medium potatoes, diced
8 fl oz (225ml) water or

Heat the vegetable oil in a heavy saucepan, add the onions and sauté until golden. Sprinkle in the cumin, coriander, ginger, turmeric and chilli powder and fry gently for 1 to 2 minutes. Add the lemon juice, chickpeas, tomatoes, potatoes and water or stock. Bring to the boil and season to taste with salt. Reduce the heat, cover and simmer for 15 minutes or until the potatoes are cooked. Serve garnished with parsley.

vegetable stock (see page
  26)
Salt to taste
Chopped fresh parsley to
  garnish

Serves 4

MOROCCAN VEGETABLE CASSEROLE WITH COUSCOUS

No two casseroles need be the same and the vegetables used in this recipe may be altered to suit what is available or in season. The cooking method is interesting, however. The Moroccans add the vegetables straight to boiling water without sautéeing them first. Towards the end of the cooking period onions and seasoning are fried together and added to the pot of vegetables. The casserole develops a better flavour than would be expected and it goes very well with couscous. In North Africa there is a lot of tradition attached to the way couscous is cooked, but it can be prepared very simply if you wish. Put the couscous into a bowl, pour over hot water to cover and leave to stand for 10 minutes. Meanwhile chop up some fresh herbs: coriander, mint or parsley for instance. Drain the couscous in a colander, mix in the fresh herbs, a little salt and it's ready!

2 pints (1.1 litres) water
2 teaspoons salt
4 to 6 cloves garlic, peeled
2 medium carrots, coarsely
  chopped
2 medium onions, diced
2 medium potatoes, chopped
1 small turnip, chopped
2 medium courgettes, thickly
  sliced
1 medium aubergine, cubed
4 tablespoons vegetable oil
1 to 2 chilli peppers, seeded
  and chopped
1 teaspoon ground cumin
2 tablespoons chopped fresh
  parsley

Put the water and salt in a large pot and bring to the boil. Add the next 7 ingredients, reserving half of the diced onion. Cover and return to the boil, reduce the heat and simmer until all the vegetables are tender. Meanwhile, heat the oil in a heavy frying pan and sauté the reserved onion, chilli peppers, cumin and parsley until the onion is soft. Pour this mixture into the vegetable pot and simmer for a further 5 minutes. With a slotted spoon lift out some of the vegetables and garnish the prepared couscous with them. Serve the garnished

1 lb (450g) couscous
(prepared as directed above)

Serves 6

couscous and the remaining vegetables from separate dishes.

GRILLED LEEKS BRUSHED WITH MISO SAUCE

This Japanese way of cooking leeks may also be used for other vegetables such as courgettes, peppers, aubergines or mushrooms.

4 leeks, sliced into 1½ in
(4cm) lengths
2 tablespoons vegetable oil
1 tablespoon miso
1 tablespoon sugar
1 tablespoon mirin or sweet
sherry

Serves 4

Preheat a medium grill. Divide the leeks between 4 skewers and brush them liberally with the oil. Combine the miso, sugar and mirin or sherry and mix well. Grill the oiled leeks, turning them often until they are lightly browned. Remove them from the grill and brush all over with the miso sauce, then grill again for about 2 minutes. The leeks will burn easily once they have been brushed with the sauce, so take care to turn them frequently.

GADO-GADO

Gado-gado is a popular Indonesian dish consisting of a mixture of raw and cooked vegetables arranged on a serving dish and served with a spicy peanut sauce either poured over them or in a side bowl. It is light, crunchy, tasty, and good for you. The vegetables suggested below may be changed to suit availability or personal preference. If you do not like moderately hot food, omit the chilli powder or use less than suggested.

Peanut Sauce
1 tablespoon vegetable oil
1 clove garlic, crushed
½ medium onion, finely diced
½ red chilli, seeds removed,
chopped, or ¼ teaspoon

To make the sauce, heat the oil in a small pan and sauté the garlic, onion and chilli pepper or hot pepper sauce until softened. Put the contents of the pan into a blender and add the peanut

hot pepper sauce
4 oz (100g) peanut butter
2 teaspoons brown sugar
2 teaspoons lemon juice
8 fl oz (225ml) water
Salt to taste

Vegetables
2 medium potatoes, chopped
4 oz (100g) French beans,
topped and tailed, and cut
into 2 ini (5cm) lengths
2 medium carrots, cut in half,
and thickly sliced lengthwise
½ medium cucumber, sliced
4 oz (100g) beansprouts,
washed and drained
½ head crisp lettuce, washed
and chopped

Serves 4 to 6

butter, sugar, lemon juice and water.
Process to a smooth sauce and then
pour back into the pan. Bring to a
gentle boil, stirring occasionally, add
salt to taste and set on a low simmer.

Boil the potatoes until just tender. Boil
the beans and carrots in salted just to
cover for 5 minutes only, then drain.
Arrange the cucumber, beansprouts,
lettuce, cooked potatoes and
parcooked French beans and carrots
on a serving dish, and serve with the
hot peanut sauce poured over or in a
separate bowl.

Variation:
For an authentic Indonesian-style
peanut sauce substitute coconut milk
(fresh or canned) for the water.

STIR-FRIED CELERY AND ALMONDS

*Celery can be braised, baked or stir-fried, but fast boiling should be
avoided as celery needs slow cooking to break down its fibrous
texture – otherwise it will taste coarse and stringy and lack flavour.
Celery is delicious made into soups or try it in this quick stir-fry
recipe.*

1 clove garlic, crushed
½ teaspoon ground cumin
4 tablespoons olive oil or
other vegetable oil
6 sticks celery, washed, cut
into 2×¼ in (5×0.6cm)
sticks
1 medium red pepper, seeded
and cut into thin strips
4 oz (100g) French beans,
topped, tailed and cut in
half

Fry the garlic and cumin in the oil in a
deep frying pan or wok for 2 to 3
minutes until the garlic turns golden.
Add the celery, red pepper and French
beans and fry, stirring occasionally,
for 8 to 10 minutes until the
vegetables are almost soft but still have
some texture. Add the thyme, salt and
black pepper to taste and half the
flaked almonds. Stir for another
minute then serve immediately with

1 tablespoon chopped fresh
  thyme, or 1 teaspoon dried
  thyme
Salt and freshly ground black
  pepper to taste
1 oz (25g) flaked almonds,
  toasted

Serves 4

the remaining almonds scattered over
the top.

STIR-FRIED WATERCRESS AND CHINESE MUSHROOMS

Watercress is most often used in Britain as a salad ingredient but the Chinese use it as a vegetable. Its good flavour and rapid cooking time make it a convenient stir-fry ingredient.

2 bunches fresh green
  watercress
6 Chinese dried black
  mushrooms
2 tablespoons vegetable oil
2 oz (50g) tinned bamboo
  shoots, shredded
Salt to taste
1 teaspoon sugar
1 in (2.5cm) piece ginger root,
  peeled and finely chopped

Serves 4 as a side dish

Trim the watercress, discarding the
tougher stems. Rinse and shake it
well. Put the mushrooms in a mixing
bowl, add boiling water to cover and
allow to stand for 30 minutes. Drain
them, then squeeze to remove excess
moisture. Cut off and discard the
tough stalks, and finely chop the
caps. Heat the oil in a frying pan or wok
and add the bamboo shoots and
mushrooms. Cook, stirring, over a
high heat for about 1 minute. Add the
watercress and stir. Add the salt, sugar
and ginger and cook for 1 minute,
stirring all the while. Spoon the
vegetables on to a serving dish, leaving
any liquid in the pan. Reduce it over a
high heat, then pour into the pan the
liquid that will have accumulated in
the serving dish (rather a lot). Reduce
briefly, and pour over the vegetables.

Mishshi (Stuffed Vegetables)

Stuffed vegetables, called *mishshi* or *dolmas*, are an intrinsic part of Arab cuisine and nearly every vegetable available to the Middle Eastern cook has been adapted to this way of cooking. There is a host of fillings and as many ways of stuffing and cooking the vegetables. To simplify matters I have given recipes for three different fillings, plus a description of how to prepare and cook a variety of vegetables suitable for stuffing. There is also a recipe for tomato sauce which may be substituted for water as the cooking medium. Thus you can select a filling and a vegetable in whichever combination appeals to you and make your own *mishshi*. Courgettes, aubergines and green or red peppers are the most common vegetables used for stuffing. Most *mishshi* can be served hot, warm or cold. If you plan to serve them warm or cold use olive oil for any frying that is required since this is the most digestible oil eaten cold. Serve with rice, salad and pickles.

RICE FILLING

In this recipe cooked rice has been used but if the vegetables you are stuffing need a long cooking time use parcooked rice, reduce the amount used to two-thirds that of the cooked rice, and pack the vegetables less tightly.

2 medium onions, finely diced
2 tablespoons vegetable oil
8 oz (225g) rice, cooked and drained
2 medium tomatoes, skinned and chopped (see page 30)
2 tablespoons chopped fresh parsley, mint or coriander
½ teaspoon allspice
½ teaspoon cinnamon
Salt and freshly ground black pepper to taste
2 oz (50g) raisins or sultanas, soaked for 30 minutes to 1 hour and drained (optional)

Lightly fry the onions in the oil, then combine with all the other ingredients and mix well.

Serves 4

RICE AND CHICKPEA FILLING

Replace half the rice in the above recipe with 8 oz (225g) cooked, drained chickpeas.

RICE AND NUT FILLING

Follow the recipe for rice filling (above) but instead of tomatoes use 4 oz (100g) nuts, e.g. pine nuts, blanched almonds, chopped walnuts, pistachios.

QUICK TOMATO SAUCE

3 tablespoons tomato purée
Juice of 2 lemons
12 fl oz (325ml) water
Salt and freshly ground black
  pepper to taste

Makes ¾ pint (450ml)

Combine all the ingredients in a pan and bring to the boil. Remove from the heat and it's ready to use.

Preparing and Cooking Stuffed Vegetables

AUBERGINES

4 medium aubergines, stalks
  left on
Salt
2 tablespoons oil

Preheat the oven to 350°F (180°C, gas mark 4).

Wash the aubergines and make a deep

Selected filling (see p.96-7)
Water or tomato sauce (see p.97)

slit from one end to the other without breaking open the end. Press open the slit and sprinkle liberally with salt. Set the aubergines aside for 30 minutes and then rinse them out and pat dry on paper towels. Heat the oil in a heavy frying pan and fry the aubergines all over until they have softened but have not lost their shape. Grease a casserole dish and put the aubergines into it, open side up. Pack them with the selected filling and pour into the dish enough water or tomato sauce to come half way up the sides of the aubergines. Bake in the preheated oven for 35 to 45 minutes or until they are soft.

COURGETTES

2 lb (900g) medium courgettes, washed
Selected filling (see p.96–7)
¾ pint (450ml) water or tomato sauce (see p.97)

Cut the stem ends off the courgettes and carefully hollow out the centre of each with an apple corer leaving an ⅛ to ¼ in (0.3 to 0.6 cm) shell (discard the centres). Soak the hollowed courgettes in salted water for 10 minutes then drain. Stuff them with the filling and then arrange them in a heavy saucepan. Add the water or tomato sauce and bring to the boil. Cover, reduce the heat and simmer for 30 minutes or until the courgettes are tender.

RED AND GREEN PEPPERS

4 medium red or green
  peppers
2 tablespoons oil
Selected filling (see p.96–7)
¾ pint (450ml) water or
  tomato sauce (see p.97)

Preheat the oven to 350°F (180°C, gas mark 4).

Cut the tops off the peppers, remove the seeds and the pith. Heat the oil in a heavy frying pan and lightly sauté the peppers all over until they are softened but still retain their shape. Stuff the peppers with the selected filling and pack them into a casserole dish. Put the tops back on the peppers and pour into the dish the water or tomato sauce. Bake in the preheated oven for 30 minutes or until the peppers are tender.

FENNEL

4 large fennel bulbs, hard
  bases cut off, washed
Selected filling (see p.96–7)
¾ pint (450ml) water or
  tomato sauce (see p.97)

Preheat the oven to 350°F (180°C, gas mark 4).

Cook the fennel in a pan of salted boiling water for 10 minutes, drain, cool and cut in half lengthwise. Place half the fennel, cut side uppermost, in a casserole dish and pile the filling on top. Carefully cover with the remaining fennel halves. Add the water or tomato sauce and bake for 30 minutes.

MARROW

1 large marrow, cut in half
   lengthwise and then
   crosswise, seeds scraped out
Selected filling (see p.96–7)
¾ pint (450ml) water or
   tomato sauce (see p.97)
Juice of 1 lemon (if using
   water)

Preheat the oven to 350°F (180°C, gas mark 4).

Put the marrow pieces into a large pan of boiling salted water and cook until the pulp is just softened. Drain them, and scoop out and discard enough pulp to leave a thick shell. Put the marrow shells into an oiled baking dish and stuff with the filling. Pour the water and lemon juice, or the tomato sauce, into the baking dish and bake in the preheated oven for 45 minutes or until the marrow and filling are tender.

TOMATOES

8 medium tomatoes
Salt and freshly ground black
   pepper to taste
Selected filling (see p.96-7)
2 tablespoons olive oil

Preheat the oven to 350°F (180°C, gas mark 4).

Cut ¼ to ½ in (0.6 to 1.25cm) tops off the tomatoes and reserve them. Carefully scoop out the tomato pulp, leaving a ½ in (1.25cm) shell. Sprinkle the inside with salt and black pepper and set aside. Chop the tomato pulp and add to the filling. Stuff the tomatoes with the filling and brush them all over with the olive oil. Put them in a shallow baking dish and replace the tops. Bake in the preheated oven for 20 minutes.

ONIONS

4 large onions, peeled
Selected filling (see p.96–7)
Juice of 1 lemon

Preheat the oven to 350°F (180°C, gas mark 4).

Cook the onions in a small amount of water over a low heat for 20 minutes. Drain and reserve the liquid. Cut a slice off the stem end of each onion and scoop out the centre, leaving a moderately thick wall. Stuff the onions with the filling. Set aside. Chop up the centres and place them in a baking dish along with the reserved liquid and the juice of 1 lemon. Pack the stuffed onions into the dish, cover and bake in the preheated oven for 1 hour. Alternatively they can be simmered, covered, over a low heat on top of the cooker for the same time.

GRAINS, PASTA AND NOODLES

Grains

Grains are the edible seeds of cereals. They are literally embryonic plants and as such are small packages of nourishment and energy. The main grains we eat in the West are rice, wheat (mainly as flour in bread, pasta and so on, but also as bulgar wheat and couscous), barley, oats, millet and buckwheat. Whole grains are an excellent source of protein, vitamins and minerals. Eaten in combination with pulses they provide particularly high-quality protein.

Purchase grains from a reputable and busy health or wholefood store to ensure they have not been kept for an overlong period. At home, store grains in airtight containers in a cool, dry place. If possible, buy organically grown grains and ensure that they are whole and unrefined.

All grains are very good cooked on their own in water and then served as a side dish to vegetables or with a sauce, or combined with raw vegetables and made into a salad. Cooked grains can also be mixed with other ingredients and baked, or used to stuff vegetables or make rissoles. Some grains benefit from dry-roasting before being boiled in water. This is particularly the case with buckwheat (kasha).

To dry-roast or toast grains, heat in a dry frying pan or saucepan over a moderate heat, stirring and shaking them until they brown lightly.

The general rules for cooking grains are as follows. Rinse the grain under the cold water tap and drain. Measure the cooking water into the pot and bring it to the boil. Add the grain, stir, add salt if you wish (1/4 to 1/2 teaspoon per 8 oz (225g) grain), and return the pot to the boil. Reduce the heat to very low. Cover and cook until the grain is tender and the water has been absorbed. Cooking times and water-to-grain ratios are given in the table below.

Grain	Water/grain ratio	Cooking time
Barley (whole)	3:1	1 hour
Buckwheat	2:1	15-20 minutes
Bulgar wheat	2:1	15-20 minutes
Millet	3:1	40-45 minutes
Rice — white	1½ to 2:1	15-20 minutes
— brown	2:1	50-60 minutes
Wholewheat berries	3:1	1½-2 hours
Cracked wheat	2:1	15-20 minutes
Wild rice	3:1	1 hour

The following approximate rules are useful:

1. 8 oz (225g) uncooked grains gives 1½ lb (675g) cooked grains.
2. One volume uncooked grains gives 3 volumes cooked grains.
3. 3 oz (75g) uncooked grains per person is an average serving.

Pasta and Noodles

Pasta Italian-style and noodles are made from a dough of wheat or other grain flour and water (other ingredients may be added such as spinach; eggs are also sometimes included so make sure any pasta or noodles you buy are egg-free). The dough is rolled out and cut into any of a huge variety of shapes, then dried before cooking in water. The best pasta is made from hard-grained wheats, particularly durum wheat.

Wholemeal pasta and noodles are more nutritious and higher in protein than the more common white flour varieties.

When cooking pasta or noodles the important rule is to use a large pot and plenty of water. Generally 1 lb (450g) pasta needs 6 pints (3.5 litres) water. Add salt after the water has boiled and before the pasta is put in – 1½ tablespoons salt per lb (450g) pasta is an average amount. To prevent the pasta sticking to itself during cooking, a little oil is added to the water. Thus, the water is brought to a rolling boil, salted, about 2 tablespoons oil are added and the pasta is then carefully fed into the pot and boiled, uncovered, until it is soft on the outside but with a slight resistance at the centre – *al dente*. Cooking times vary depending on the type of pasta and whether it is bought or homemade. As soon as the pasta is cooked, drain it in a colander and serve with a sauce or on its own with olive oil and freshly milled black pepper.

POLENTA

Polenta is a semolina lookalike but it is made from corn rather than wheat grain. In Italy it is cooked into a stiff yellow porridge and served hot – often with a garlicky tomato sauce – or cooled, cut into wedges and fried. Serve with vegetables and/or a salad.

1¾ pints (1 litre) water
8 oz (225g) polenta
Salt and freshly ground black
  pepper
Olive oil

Put the water in a large pan, add salt and bring to a gentle boil. Pour the polenta slowly into the water and stir continuously. Reduce the heat to the

Serves 4 to 6

lowest setting and cook, stirring, for 20 minutes, or according to the directions on the packet. Once ready the polenta will come away from the sides of the pan. Serve immediately with a sauce of your choice or simply sprinkled with black pepper and olive oil. Alternatively pour the polenta into an oiled frying pan or other shallow dish. Smooth the top then brush with a little olive oil and leave to cool or until solid. Turn the wheel of polenta out of the pan and cut it into wedges. Return the wedges to the pan and fry in olive oil for about 5 minutes each side. Serve as for freshly cooked polenta.

INDONESIAN FRIED RICE

2 tablespoons vegetable oil
1 medium onion, sliced
1 clove garlic, crushed
1 or 2 fresh or dried red chillies, finely chopped, or ½ to 1 teaspoon chilli powder
8 oz (225g) rice, cooked and drained
1 tablespoon dark soya sauce
½ teaspoon brown sugar
Salt to taste

Garnish
Tomato wedges
Cucumber slices

Serves 4

Heat the oil in a heavy frying pan or wok, add the onion, garlic and chillies and stir-fry them for about 1 minute. Add the rice, soya sauce and brown sugar. Mix well and cook, stirring continuously, over a moderate heat for 5 to 6 minutes. During this time check the rice for seasoning and add salt if needed. If the mixture starts to look too dry, add a little more vegetable oil. Serve the fried rice immediately on a large serving dish or individual plates and garnish it with tomato wedges and cucumber slices.

MIDDLE EASTERN RICE STEW WITH LEMON AND VEGETABLES

A colourful, nutritious and very tasty one-course meal.

2 tablespoons vegetable oil
3 medium onions, thinly sliced
3 tablespoons split red lentils
8 oz (225g) rice
2 pints (1.1 litres) water
1 lb (450g) spinach, chopped
1 teaspoon coriander seeds
1 tablespoon chopped fresh
  parsley
Salt and freshly ground black
  pepper to taste
Juice of 2 lemons

Garnish
1 medium onion, diced
1 tablespoon vegetable oil
1 teaspoon dried mint

Serves 4

Heat the oil in a heavy pan, add the sliced onions and sauté until lightly browned. Stir in the lentils and the rice, add the water and bring to the boil. Reduce the heat, cover and simmer for 20 minutes. Now add the spinach, coriander, parsley and salt and black pepper to taste, and continue cooking a further 30 minutes. Meanwhile make the garnish: fry the diced onion in the oil until well-browned, sprinkle on the mint and fry a further minute. Pour the stew into a serving bowl, stir in the lemon juice, garnish with the mint and fried onion and serve.

OAT OR ADUKI BEAN HOTPOT

This dish combines beans, oats, vegetables and apples. It's tasty, well-balanced and nutritious.

12 oz (350g) aduki beans
2 pints (1.1 litres) water
2 medium onions, chopped
4 oz (100g) carrots, chopped
4 sticks celery, chopped
2 tablespoons oil
2 apples, cored and thinly
  sliced
2 bay leaves
Salt and freshly ground black
  pepper to taste
3 oz (75g) oats

Serves 4

Soak the beans in the water for 2 to 3 hours and then gently boil in the same water for 1 hour. Sauté the onions, carrots and celery in the oil until just soft. Add the sautéed vegetables, the apples, bay leaves and seasoning to the beans and their cooking water. Bring to the boil and simmer for 30 minutes. Add the oats to the pot, simmer for a further 10 minutes and serve.

IRANIAN CHELO RICE

Rice cooked in this fashion, known as chelo *rice, is served with one of a variety of Iranian sauces called* khoreshe, *for which a recipe follows.*

12 oz (350g) basmati or long grain rice, soaked in water for 4 to 6 hours or overnight
1 tablespoon salt
4 pints (2.2 litres) water
3 oz (75g) vegetable margarine, melted

Serves 4

Drain the rice well and wash it under running cold water until the water runs clear. Drain again. Bring the salt and water to the boil and gradually stir in the rice. Return to the boil and boil rapidly for 8 minutes or until the rice is not quite tender. At this stage the centre of a rice grain should not be hard, but the rice should still be a little chewy. Strain the rice, rinse with a little warm water and leave to drain thoroughly. Put 1 tablespoon of the melted margarine and 2 tablespoons of water in a heavy pan. Mound the rice into the pan, forming a rough cone shape. Make a hole down the centre of the cone with the handle of a wooden spoon and pour down the hole the remaining melted margarine. Wrap the lid of the saucepan in a clean tea towel, keeping the ends well tucked in, and put the lid on. The towel absorbs any rising steam and the rice grains stay fluffy and separate. Put the pan on a low heat and simmer for 20 to 25 minutes.

The rice at the bottom of the pan forms a golden crust which can be scraped off and served as a delicacy on its own or used to garnish the rice.

VEGETABLE AND LEMON KHORESHE

2 oz (50g) vegetable margarine
1 medium onion, thinly sliced
2 medium carrots, cut into 1 in (2.5cm) matchsticks
4 oz (100g) green beans, fresh or frozen, cut in 1 in (2.5cm) lengths
2 oz (50g) nuts (almonds, pine nuts, pistachios, walnuts etc), chopped
Juice and grated rind of 1 lemon
1 teaspoon ground cinnamon
½ teaspoon ground nutmeg
Salt and freshly ground black pepper to taste
1 lb (450g) cooked *chelo* rice (see recipe above) or plain cooked rice

Melt the margarine in a heavy pan and sauté the onion and carrots over a moderate heat. Cook, stirring occasionally for 5 minutes. Add all the remaining ingredients except the rice, mix well, bring to the boil, reduce heat, cover and simmer for 30 minutes, stirring occasionally. Serve in a separate bowl from the cooked rice.

Serves 4

JAPANESE FRIED RICE

2 tablespoons vegetable oil
1 clove garlic, crushed
1 medium onion, diced
4 oz (100g) mushrooms, sliced
4 oz (100g) celery or French beans, chopped
1 lb (450g) (cooked weight) cooked rice
6 oz (175g) pressed beancurd (see page 22), cut into 1 in (2.5cm) cubes
2 tablespoons soya sauce

Heat the oil in a heavy frying pan. Add the crushed garlic and onion. Sauté until the onion is just soft, and then add the mushrooms and celery or French beans. Fry gently for 2 or 3 minutes, retaining the texture of each vegetable. Stir in the rice and beancurd. Heat through, stirring constantly, sprinkle on the soya sauce and mix well. Serve.

Serves 4

YELLOW RICE WITH COCONUT MILK

In this Indonesian recipe the rice is coloured yellow with turmeric and cooked in coconut milk instead of water. The finished rice should be colourfully garnished. It makes a bright, rich centrepiece to a special meal. For yellow rice cooked without coconut milk see the recipe for Sultan's pilav below.

1 lb (450g) long grain rice, washed several times and drained
1 pint (550ml) coconut milk
1 teaspoon ground turmeric
1 bay leaf
½ teaspoon salt

Garnish
Choose from:
Onion slices, fried until brown
Finely sliced cucumber
Fresh chilli peppers, deseeded and chopped

Serves 4 to 6

Put the rice in a bowl, cover with water and leave to soak for 2 or 3 hours. Drain and then put into a heavy-bottomed pan with the other ingredients. Bring to a gentle boil and cook over a low heat, uncovered, until all the coconut milk has been absorbed. Now stir the rice with the handle end of a wooden spoon and then cover the pot with a tightly fitting lid. Reduce the heat to the lowest setting possible and gently cook the rice for another 15 minutes. Tip it into a serving bowl, garnish and serve.

SULTAN'S PILAV

This Turkish dish is traditionally made with pistachio nuts but you can equally well substitute pine nuts or even chopped walnuts or cashews.

4 oz (100g) vegetable margarine
1 lb (450g) long grain rice, washed thoroughly and drained
1¼ pints (700ml) water or vegetable stock (see page 26)
2 oz (50g) sultanas, soaked for 1 hour and drained
Pinch of saffron or turmeric
½ teaspoon allspice

Melt the margarine in a heavy saucepan. Add the rice and sauté, stirring, until each grain is coated in fat. Add the remaining ingredients, except for 1 tablespoon of the nuts, and bring the mixture to the boil. Reduce the heat, cover the pan with a tight-fitting lid and simmer for 20 minutes. Remove the pan from the heat and allow to stand for 10 minutes. Meanwhile lightly toast and

2 oz (50g) pistachios or other nuts

Salt and freshly ground black pepper to taste

Serves 4

then finely chop the reserved nuts. Tip the pilav on to a serving dish and garnish with the chopped, toasted nuts.

RED RICE

Rice and aduki beans eaten together provide a rich protein source as well as a colourful dish.

4 oz (100g) aduki beans, soaked in water for 6 hours or more

2 pints (1.1 litres) water

1 lb (450g) brown rice, washed and drained

1 teaspoon salt

2 tablespoons sesame seeds, dry-roasted (see page 18)

Serves 4

Drain the soaked beans. Place them in a pot with the water, bring to the boil, reduce the heat, then cover and simmer until cooked (about 1½ hours). Drain and reserve the liquid. Put the rice in the pot, add more water to the bean cooking liquid to make 1½ pints (825ml) and add to the rice. Cover and bring to the boil. Reduce the heat and simmer, covered, for 30 minutes. Now add the beans, mix well and continue to simmer until the rice is cooked (about 20 minutes). Combine the salt and toasted sesame seeds. Serve the red rice hot or cold, garnished with the sesame seed and salt mixture (a Japanese condiment known as *gomashio*).

VEGETABLE PAELLA

Paella is a famous Spanish dish named after the large flat pan with two handles in which it is cooked. The pan doubles as a serving dish. A large frying pan and a serving dish do the job just as well, although a little of the drama of bringing the food straight from the stove to the table is lost.

3 tablespoons vegetable oil
2 cloves garlic, crushed
2 medium onions, sliced
2 medium green peppers, cored, seeded and sliced
2 medium tomatoes, chopped
12 oz (350g) long grain brown rice
1½ pints (825ml) water or vegetable stock (see page 26)
Salt and freshly ground black pepper to taste
4 oz (100g) cucumber, peeled and diced
2 sticks celery, chopped
4 oz (100g) nuts, chopped
2 oz (50g) olives (optional)

Serves 6

Heat the oil in a heavy frying pan and sauté the garlic and onions until they start to colour. Add the peppers and sauté for a further 2 to 3 minutes. Stir in the tomatoes and rice and cook over a low heat, stirring, for 5 minutes. Pour in the water or stock, season to taste with salt and black pepper and boil rapidly for 5 minutes. Add the cucumber, celery and chopped nuts, reduce the heat to a simmer and cook until the rice is tender and all the liquid is absorbed. Add more water if the rice dries up before it is tender. Serve garnished with olives, if liked.

BROWN RICE WITH MUSHROOMS

Serve with stir-fried vegetables for a no-fuss nutritious meal.

2 tablespoons vegetable oil (sesame oil goes well)
2 medium onions, chopped
8 oz (225g) mushrooms, chopped
12 oz (350g) brown rice, washed and drained
1½ pints (825ml) boiling water
1 tablespoon soya sauce

Serves 4

Preheat the oven to 325°F (170°C, gas mark 3).

Heat the oil in a heavy frying pan, add the onions and fry until they are just soft. Stir in the mushrooms and cook for a further 2 minutes. Combine the onions and mushrooms with the rice in an ovenproof casserole and add the water and soya sauce. Cover and bake for 1 hour or until the rice is tender.

SESAME RICE AND BEANSPROUTS

A delicious vitamin- and mineral-packed rice dish. Serve with a salad for a nutritionally balanced meal.

12 oz (350g) rice, washed and drained
1 tablespoon vegetable oil (sesame oil for preference)
1 clove garlic, finely chopped
½ medium onion, finely chopped
1½ tablespoons tahini (sesame paste)
6 oz (175g) beansprouts
2 tablespoons soya sauce

Serves 4

Cook the rice. Meanwhile, heat the oil in a wok or frying pan and sauté the garlic and onion until golden. Stir in the tahini and then the beansprouts. Stir-fry until the beansprouts are very hot. Stir the mixture and the soya sauce into the hot, cooked, drained rice and serve.

SPICED RICE

The Indonesian name for this dish, nasi gemuk, *means rice cooked in oil. First the spices are fried in oil, then raw rice is stirred in, liquid – traditionally coconut milk – is added, and the mixture is simmered until the rice is cooked.*

3 tablespoons vegetable oil
1 in (2.5cm) piece of cinnamon
1 clove
2 cardamom pods, broken open
1 small onion, finely diced
2 cloves garlic, crushed
½ in (1cm) piece ginger root, finely chopped
½ teaspoon ground coriander
1 lb (450g) long grain rice, washed several times and drained
Salt to taste
1¼ pints (700ml) water, vegetable stock (see page 26) or coconut milk

Serves 4 to 6

Heat the oil in a heavy saucepan or wok and add the cinnamon, clove and cardamom pods. Fry for 1 or 2 minutes. Add the onion, garlic, ginger and coriander and stir-fry for another 1 or 2 minutes. Stir the rice into the spice mixture and add salt to taste. Carefully pour in the water, stock or coconut milk and bring the rice to the boil. Cover, reduce the heat and simmer for 15 to 20 minutes or until the rice is tender.

Variation
If you like chilli-hot dishes, add 1 or 2 finely chopped chillies with the onion and garlic.

CHESTNUT RICE

15 to 20 fresh chestnuts
2 tablespoons soya sauce
2 tablespoons sake or
  medium-sweet white wine
1 lb (450g) rice, washed and
  drained
2 volumes of water to 1
  volume of rice
1 tablespoon sesame seeds,
  dry-roasted (see page 18)

Serves 4 to 6

Make a criss-cross incision in the shells of the chestnuts with a sharp knife and boil them in water for 5 minutes. Drain the chestnuts, rinse them under cold water, peel them and cut into quarters. Combine the chestnuts, soya sauce, sake or wine, rice and water and cook until tender and the water has been absorbed. Serve sprinkled with the roasted sesame seeds.

FAST COUSCOUS

Traditionally, making couscous was a long-winded business in which the couscous grain was slowly steamed over a sauce of meat and vegetables. However, nowadays most couscous sold in shops, even in North America, is the quick-cooking variety and it will cook within five minutes, once covered in boiling water. Of course one may still cook it in the traditional way but this new convenience makes it a practical grain to use in place of, say, rice. It is delicious and often enjoyed by children who otherwise dislike grain dishes.

1 tablespoon olive oil
1 medium onion, sliced
2 cloves garlic, crushed
2 medium carrots, coarsely
  chopped (or 2 medium
  potatoes, coarsely chopped)
1 medium green pepper, cored
  and thickly sliced
2 medium courgettes, thickly
  sliced
14 oz (400g) tinned tomatoes
2 oz (50g) almonds or pine
  nuts
4 oz (100g) sultanas or dried
  apricots (chopped),

Heat the oil in a large pan, add the onion and garlic, stir and cook for 2 or 3 minutes. Add the carrots or potatoes, green pepper and courgettes. Stir and cook for another 2 or 3 minutes. Add the tomatoes, almonds or pinenuts, sultanas or apricots, hot pepper sauce and salt to taste. Add water to cover, bring to the boil, cover the pan, reduce the heat and simmer for 10 minutes. After 5 minutes pour the boiling water over the couscous and leave to stand for 5 minutes. Make a bed of the couscous in a

plumped up in a little
boiling water
1 teaspoon hot pepper sauce
(or harissa)
Salt to taste
10 oz (275g) couscous
1¾ pints (1 litre) boiling water

Serves 4

serving dish (if it is lumpy separate the
grains using your fingers). Pour the
vegetables and sauce over the top and
serve. Provide extra hot pepper sauce
for those who like it.

COURGETTES TABBOULEH WITH
HAZELNUT SAUCE

---

*The filling for the courgettes is very similar to the traditional Arab
salad, tabbouleh. It combines deliciously with the nut sauce.*

4 oz (100g) bulgar wheat
4 medium courgettes
1 bunch spring onions
1 tablespoon olive oil
2 cloves garlic, crushed
2 medium tomatoes, deseeded
and chopped
2 tablespoons chopped fresh
mint
1 tablespoon chopped fresh
parsley
Salt and freshly ground black
pepper to taste
Juice of 1 lemon

Sauce
4 oz (100g) ground hazelnuts
(or walnuts)
4 cloves garlic, crushed
2 tablespoons fresh
breadcrumbs
½ teaspoon salt
2 tablespoons olive oil
Juice of 1 lemon
⅓ pint (200ml) water

Serves 4

Preheat the oven to 325°F (170°C, gas
mark 3).

Soak the wheat in very hot water for
about 15 minutes or until swollen.
Meanwhile blanch the courgettes
whole in boiling, lightly salted water
for 3 to 4 minutes. Cut them
lengthways, scoop out the centres and
reserve. Chop the white parts and a
little of the green parts of the spring
onions and sweat them gently in the
oil. After a few minutes add the
chopped courgette centres, the garlic
and the tomatoes. Mix in the wheat,
the fresh mint and parsley, and
seasoning. Remove from the heat and
add the lemon juice.

To make the sauce, blend all the
ingredients together and allow to
stand for at least 30 minutes.

To assemble: arrange the 8 courgette
shells in an ovenproof dish and fill
them with the wheat mixture. Heat
the sauce and either serve it separately

or pour it into the dish with the courgettes. Bake the courgettes in the preheated oven for 15 minutes.

CRACKED WHEAT AND OKRA PILAV

Cracked wheat is a similar product to bulgar wheat but there is no parboiling process in its manufacture. It thus takes a little longer to cook than bulgar wheat.

2 tablespoons vegetable oil
4 or 6 okra pods, washed well, stalk ends trimmed off
2 small courgettes, sliced into ½ in (1.25cm) rounds
1 red pepper, cored, seeded and finely chopped
1 medium stick celery, finely chopped
1 bay leaf
¾ pint (450ml) vegetable stock (see page 26) or water
6 oz (175g) cracked wheat
Salt and freshly ground black pepper to taste

Serves 4

Heat the oil in a heavy saucepan and add all the vegetables. Sauté them over a medium heat for 5 minutes. Add the bay leaf and the stock or water and bring to the boil. Lower the heat and simmer for 5 minutes. Add the cracked wheat and salt and black pepper to taste and bring to the boil again, then reduce the heat to very low and simmer for 15 minutes. Look inside the pot after 10 minutes and leave uncovered if the wheat is too moist.

LEEKS WITH NOODLES

Simple to make. Wholesome and filling to eat.

4 medium leeks, washed and sliced into ½ in (1.25cm) pieces
3 oz (75g) vegetable margarine
5 oz (150g) mushrooms, sliced
Salt and freshly ground black pepper to taste
12 oz (350g) noodles
3 oz (75g) breadcrumbs

Sauté the leeks in the margarine until soft and transparent. Add the sliced mushrooms and cook for a further 5 minutes. Season to taste with salt and black pepper. Boil the noodles in plenty of salted water for 5 to 7 minutes or until *al dente*. Drain and mix with the leeks and mushrooms.

Serves 4

Put in a dish, sprinkle over the breadcrumbs, and flash under a hot grill until the breadcrumbs are crisp and golden. Serve at once.

TOSSED NOODLES WITH VEGETABLES AND NUTS

Once the noodles are cooked this Chinese stir-fry dish is very quick to prepare. Red bean paste is readily available at any Chinese grocery store.

2 tablespoons vegetable oil
1 or 2 green chillies, seeded and finely chopped
1 clove garlic, finely chopped
6 oz (175g) cashew nuts
½ medium cucumber, chopped into matchsticks
2 carrots, chopped into matchsticks
3 sticks celery, finely sliced
4 spring onions, sliced
6 oz (175g) button mushrooms, whole
1 small green pepper, seeded and sliced
1 tablespoon soya sauce
2 tablespoons sweet red bean paste
1 tablespoon dry sherry
12 oz (350g) noodles, cooked, rinsed under cold water and set aside

Serves 4 to 6

Heat the oil in a wok or deep frying pan, add the chillies and garlic and fry quickly for about 30 seconds. Add the cashew nuts and cook for 2 minutes. Increase the heat, add all the vegetables and cook for 1 minute more. Stir in the soya sauce, bean paste, sherry and then the noodles. Turn and stir well to mix and heat through. Pile into a large warmed dish and serve immediately.

INDIAN SUMMER NOODLES

This is a spicy dish using homegrown vegetables readily available in late summer and early autumn. It makes a good, one-pot meal.

8 oz (225g) wide noodles
1 tablespoon vegetable oil
2 oz (50g) vegetable margarine
2 cloves garlic, finely chopped
2 teaspoons ground coriander
1 lb (450g) tomatoes, thinly
    sliced
2 teaspoons black onion seeds
    (optional – usually available
    from Indian grocers)
¼ to ½ level teaspoon
    cayenne pepper
1 lb (450g) courgettes,
    chopped into 1 in (2.5cm)
    pieces
2 teaspoons soft brown sugar
1 bunch fresh coriander,
    separate leaves from stems,
    discard the stems or use to
    make stock

Serves 4

First break up the noodles so that they are in roughly 2 in (5cm) lengths. Then cook them in boiling salted water until tender, drain, and transfer to a bowl. Stir a little oil into the noodles to stop them sticking together, and set aside. In a large, deep frying pan or casserole heat the oil over a medium heat with 1 oz (25g) of the margarine. Add the garlic and ground coriander and stir around for a minute. Then add the tomatoes, onion seeds (if using), cayenne pepper and courgettes and stir over the heat for about 5 minutes until the courgettes are just cooked but still slightly crunchy. Now add the sugar, the remaining margarine and the reserved noodles. Stir for another minute or so until the margarine is melted. Finally, remove from the heat, stir in the coriander leaves, transfer to a heated serving dish and serve at once.

LENTILS WITH WHOLEWHEAT NOODLES

A Middle Eastern dish using the traditional spices cumin and coriander. There is an oven-baked variation given below.

2 tablespoons vegetable oil
1 large onion, diced
2 cloves garlic, crushed
½ teaspoon ground cumin
½ teaspoon ground coriander
8 oz (225g) whole lentils,
    cooked and drained
Salt and freshly ground black
    pepper to taste
8 oz (225g) wholewheat
    noodles (or spaghetti),
    cooked and drained

Pour the oil into a large saucepan and add the onion and garlic. Sauté until golden. Add the cumin and coriander and toss in the lentils. Stir well and heat through. Season to taste with salt and black pepper. Add the freshly cooked noodles and mix gently. Heat through over a low flame. Transfer the mixture to a warmed serving dish and serve.

Serves 4

Variation
Layer the onion mixture, lentils and
noodles in a baking dish and pour a
tomato sauce (see page 30) over the
dish. Bake in a preheated oven at
375°F (190°c, gas mark 5) for 20
minutes.

SOFT FRIED NOODLES WITH VEGETABLES

*You may use any conveniently available noodles in this simple
Chinese recipe.*

12 oz (350g) noodles
3 tablespoons oil
1 clove garlic, crushed
1 tablespoon grated ginger
  root
½ medium carrot, peeled and
  grated
4 oz (100g) Chinese cabbage,
  shredded
1 medium green pepper,
  cored, seeded and diced
Freshly ground black pepper
  and soya sauce to taste

Serves 4

Cook the noodles in plenty of boiling
water until tender but still just firm at
the core (*al dente*). Drain and rinse
under lots of cold water. Drain again
and stir in 1 tablespoon of the oil.
Heat the remaining oil in a large
frying pan or wok and sauté the garlic
and ginger for 2 or 3 minutes. Add the
carrot, cabbage and green pepper and
sauté until they are just softened. Stir
in the noodles and heat through,
stirring constantly. Season to taste
with black pepper and soya sauce and
serve.

BUCKWHEAT NOODLES WITH DIPPING SAUCE

This is a Japanese recipe in which buckwheat noodles, called soba *in
Japan, are served with a separate dipping sauce. Ordinary wheatflour
noodles may be substituted if* soba *noodles are unavailable.*

12 oz (350g) *soba* noodles
4 tablespoons soya sauce
2 tablespoons mirin or sweet
  sherry

Cook the noodles in plenty of boiling
water until *al dente*. Meanwhile, in a
small pan combine the soya sauce,
mirin or sherry, vegetable stock, miso

12 fl oz (325ml) vegetable
stock (see page 26)
1 tablespoon miso
2 tablespoons dry-roasted
sesame seeds (see page 18),
crushed to a paste, or 1
tablespoon tahini
2 tablespoons finely chopped
spring onions, chives or
young leeks

Serves 4

and sesame seed paste or tahini and
bring the mixture to the boil. Place the
soba on one large plate or in a bowl.
Divide the sauce among 4 bowls and
garnish each with the spring onions,
chives or leeks. Dip the noodles into
the sauce before eating. Both noodles
and sauce can also be served cold. The
other way to serve the dish is to divide
the noodles among 4 bowls, pour over
the sauce and garnish.

SIMPLE SPAGHETTI WITH BASIL-TOMATO SAUCE

1 lb (450g) firm but ripe fresh
tomatoes
1 lb (450g) wholemeal or
plain spaghetti
Several sprigs of basil, finely
chopped
Salt and freshly ground black
pepper to taste
2 tablespoons olive oil

Serves 4 to 6

Bring a large pan of salted water to
the boil. Put the tomatoes in a sieve,
plunge them just briefly into the water,
then remove. Now add the pasta to the
water and cook until *al dente*, stirring
occasionally with a wooden spoon.
Skin the tomatoes and dice into small
pieces. Drain the pasta and put in a
serving bowl. Add the basil, diced
tomatoes and any seeds or juice, salt
and pepper to taste and olive oil. Turn
the spaghetti until well covered with
sauce. Serve immediately.

TAGLIATELLE WITH COURGETTE SAUCE

1 large clove garlic, crushed
1 onion, chopped
3 sticks celery, chopped
8 oz (225g) courgettes,
topped, tailed and sliced
3 tablespoons vegetable oil

Fry the garlic, onion, celery and
courgettes gently in the oil for 10
minutes. Add the tomatoes and
continue cooking until they have
broken down into a pulp. Meanwhile
cook the tagliatelle according to the

12 oz (350g) fresh tomatoes,
  chopped
8 oz (225g) wholewheat
  tagliatelle
Salt and freshly ground black
  pepper to taste
1 oz (25g) whole blanched
  almonds, dry-roasted (see
  page 18)

Serves 4

instructions on the packet. Simmer the sauce for 5 minutes, then add seasoning to taste. Pour the sauce over the well-drained tagliatelle. Sprinkle with almonds and serve.

PASTA WITH BROCCOLI AND CHILLI

A delicious Italian dish with a spicy taste and attractive appearance. Cauliflower could be substituted for broccoli.

1½ lb (675g) broccoli
12 oz (350g) short macaroni
4 tablespoons olive oil
1 clove garlic, finely chopped
2 oz (50g) walnuts, broken
  into pieces
4 oz (100g) green olives
1 red chilli pepper, finely
  chopped
6 tablespoons toasted
  breadcrumbs

Serves 6

Trim and cut the broccoli into florets. Boil in plenty of salted water until tender, then drain, reserving the cooking water. Use the water to cook the pasta for 10 to 12 minutes. While the pasta cooks, heat the oil with the garlic in a small pan until the aroma arises, then add the walnuts and mix well. Drain the pasta and mix quickly with the walnuts and garlic. Add the olives, pitted if preferred, broccoli and chilli pepper. Serve sprinkled with the breadcrumbs.

GREEN LASAGNE WITH AUBERGINE AND TOMATO SAUCE

This rich main dish is best served with a crunchy green salad.

1 lb (450g) aubergines, sliced
  and then cut into 2 in × 1
  in (5cm × 2.5cm) strips
Salt
4 fl oz (100ml) olive oil

Preheat the oven to 400°F (200°C, gas mark 6).

Sprinkle the aubergine strips with salt, put in a colander or sieve, weight

8 oz (225g) onions, chopped

1 lb 12 oz (800g) tinned tomatoes, drained and chopped

2 oz (50g) fresh herbs, chopped, or 2 teaspoons mixed dried herbs

Freshly ground black pepper to taste

10 oz (275g) oven-ready green lasagne

3 oz (75g) fresh brown breadcrumbs

Serves 4

lightly with a plate and leave for 30 minutes. Rinse and squeeze to eliminate the excess moisture. Fry in 3 fl oz (75ml) of the olive oil until crisp and brown. Remove from the pan and drain on absorbent kitchen paper. Add the onions to the oil left in the pan and gently fry for about 10 minutes without browning. Add the tinned tomatoes and cook for a further 5 minutes. Allow to cool slightly, liquidize then return to the pan and reheat. Add the aubergine pieces and the herbs. Season to taste with ground black pepper and cook for 5 minutes.

Grease a large, shallow, ovenproof dish with olive oil. Cover the base with a thick layer of the sauce, then put a layer of lasagne on top. Continue until both the lasagne and the sauce are used up. Sprinkle the breadcrumbs over the top and drizzle with the remaining 1 fl oz (25ml) olive oil. Bake for 40 to 45 minutes until brown and bubbling. Cover with foil if the top gets too brown before it is cooked.

PASTA BOWS WITH MUSHROOMS AND OLIVE OIL

Wine, lemon juice and olives give this dish a sharp, tangy flavour, mellowed by the sweetness of tomato purée.

1 lb (450g) mushrooms, sliced

2 cloves garlic, crushed

3 fl oz (75ml) olive oil

4 oz (100g) black olives, stoned and chopped

2 tablespoons tomato purée

Fry the mushrooms with the garlic in the olive oil for 2 or 3 minutes. Add the olives, diluted tomato purée, wine and sugar, heat through for a few minutes, then add the lemon juice. Cook the pasta bows in plenty of

made up to ¼ pint (150ml)
with water
2 tablespoons white wine
½ teaspoon sugar
Juice of 1 lemon
12 oz (350g) pasta bows
2 tablespoons chopped fresh
parsley
2 to 3 spring onions, chopped

Serves 4

boiling, salted water until just tender.
Drain. Serve with the mushroom and
olive sauce, garnished with the parsley
and spring onions.

SPAGHETTI WITH KOHLRABI SAUCE

*Kohlrabi releases its full flavour when cooked until tender and soft.
It is at its best when small, as the bigger roots are often woody.
Small turnips may be substituted.*

1 lb (450g) kohlrabi, sliced
and quartered
1 medium onion, chopped
5 tablespoons olive oil
1 tablespoon chopped fresh
parsley
½ teaspoon dried dill
1 teaspoon dried thyme
1 bulb fennel, chopped
1 oz (25g) plain flour
Salt and ground white pepper
to taste
12 oz (350g) spaghetti

Serves 4

Fry the kohlrabi and the onion in the
olive oil until soft and lightly
browned. Add the herbs and the
fennel, then add the flour, stirring well
until it coats all the vegetables. Pour in
1 pint (550ml) cold water, bring to the
boil, reduce to a simmer, and cook
slowly until the kohlrabi is very tender
(20 to 30 minutes). Season and
liquidize. Return to the pan and
simmer while the spaghetti cooks.
Drain the spaghetti, toss in a little
olive oil and serve with the sauce.

BREADS

Wheat, which has been called the queen of grains, is one of the world's vital foods, and bread made from wheat flour is an intrinsic part of every meal for many people of the world. The success of wheat as a food crop results from the wide climatic range under which it can be grown, the nutritional value of the wheat grain and, of course, the beautiful bread it makes.

The recipes given here are for leavened (yeasted) and unleavened breads. The breads range from the traditional British wholemeal loaf to the slightly leavened, flat, round breads of the Middle East.

Leavened (Yeasted) Bread

Leavened bread can be made from any sort of wheat flour, but to make bread with a fine texture and a good satisfying taste it is best to use hard (also called strong) flour. These are flours with a high gluten content and they give a firm, elastic dough. You may use either strong brown or strong white flour, depending upon your preference and the type of bread you wish to make. Stoneground 100 per cent wholemeal flour makes the most nutritious and filling bread. For a lighter, less chewy bread, but one which still retains most of the goodness of the wheat, use wheatmeal of 81 to 85 per cent extraction. When you wish to make a light-textured bread, use a strong white flour of a low extraction.

There is no magic attached to breadmaking, and as long as you know what you are doing and why, there is no reason why every homebaking session shouldn't be a success. Below is a simple description of the various stages involved in making bread and why they are needed.

Yeast is mixed with water then it is fed some sugar to initiate the process that produces the gas carbon dioxide which causes the dough to rise. The yeast/sugar mixture starts to bubble and it is then mixed with flour, a little salt and enough water to give a firm dough. The yeast enzymes start to feed on the sugar in the flour itself, the water hydrates the protein in the flour to form gluten, and the salt encourages enzyme activity. The gluten forms a matrix which is expanded by the carbon dioxide to give a spongy dough full of air. After the dough is made it is kneaded. This has a twofold purpose: kneading improves the elasticity of the gluten and it redistributes the yeast evenly throughout the dough, producing fresh sites for enzyme activity. After kneading, the dough is allowed to rise to double its original volume then punched down and shaped into loaves before being placed in tins to rise one more time. The timing here is important since if the process takes too long the dough loses its elasticity and the texture of the bread is uneven. On the other hand, if the process is cut short, the gluten remains unstretched and the bread will be heavier than it should be. In the final stage of the operation, the bread is placed in the oven to bake. The heat kills the yeast and stops further activity, expands the gas in the dough and sets the starch and proteins. This combined activity produces a firm but airy bread.

Below is a recipe for a basic wholemeal bread, followed by suggestions for other breads in which part of the wholemeal flour is replaced by other flours.

BASIC WHOLEMEAL BREAD

This bread keeps well, and it can be used for up to one week after baking. All wholemeal flours do not bake in the same way, so do experiment with different brands of flour (and with the given recipe) until the bread you make is exactly to your liking.

2 teaspoons brown sugar
¾ oz (20g) fresh yeast, or 1 level tablespoon active dried yeast
¾ pint (450ml) slightly warm water
1½ lb (675g) wholemeal flour
1 tablespoon salt
1 tablespoon vegetable oil
Cracked wheat or sesame seeds (optional)

Makes 2 1 lb (450g) loaves

Mix the sugar, yeast and a little of the water to a smooth paste in a small bowl and set aside in a warm place until the mixture has frothed up (approximately 15 minutes). Put the flour and salt into a large mixing bowl, add the yeast mixture, oil and remaining water. Mix well, then knead the mixture until you have a smooth springy dough that comes away from the sides of the bowl. Turn the dough on to a floured board and knead well for about 5 minutes (longer if you have strong arms). Wash, dry and slightly grease the mixing bowl, place the dough in it, cover with a warm damp cloth and set it aside in a warm place for 1 to 1½ hours until risen to double its original size. Knead the dough again for 5 minutes and then divide it into 2 equal parts. Shape the dough pieces and place them into 2 lightly oiled 1 lb (450g) bread tins. Sprinkle the cracked wheat or sesame seeds, if using, on to the top of each loaf, cover the tins with a warm, damp cloth and leave them in a warm place for 30 to 45 minutes, or until the dough has risen to the top of the tins. Meanwhile preheat the oven to 425°F (220°C, gas mark 7). Place the tins in the centre of the oven and bake for 40 minutes. Remove the bread from the oven, tip the loaves out of the tins and knock the underside. If the bread sounds hollow like a drum it is cooked. If not, return the loaves, upside down, to the oven and bake for a further 10 minutes at 375°F (190°C, gas mark 5). Leave the bread to cook on a wire rack, or resting across the tops of the empty bread tins.

Variation

To prepare a variety of different breads you may replace part of the wholemeal flour in the above recipe with the following substitutes. (The comments in brackets describe the probable differences between bread made with the basic recipe and breads with the substitutes.)

8 oz – 1 lb (225g-450g) unbleached strong white flour (lighter)
4 oz – 8 oz (100g-225g) cornmeal (slightly crunchier)
8 oz – 12 oz (225g-350g) rye flour (more moist and compact)
4 oz (100g) buckwheat flour (stronger flavour)
4 oz – 8 oz (100g-225g) soya flour (adds to the protein content and gives more flavour)
4 oz – 8 oz (100g-225g) oat flour or rolled oats (adds to the protein content, chewier and more moist)

HIGH-PROTEIN BREAD

In this recipe, which is another variation of the basic wholemeal bread recipe, a portion of the wholemeal flour is replaced by a mixture of ingredients rich in protein, vitamins and minerals. The finished bread is close-textured, easy to slice and excellent for sandwiches or toast.

Replace the flour in the basic wholemeal bread recipe with the following mixture:

1 lb (450g) wholemeal flour
2 oz (50g) soya flour
1 oz (25g) wheat germ
1 oz (25g) rolled oats soaked
   in 4 fl oz (100ml) boiling
   water and allowed to cool.

Combine the ingredients in a mixing bowl and stir well, then proceed as directed in the wholemeal bread recipe.

BASIC UNLEAVENED BREAD (WITHOUT YEAST)

Unyeasted bread is heavier than the risen variety, so it is better to cut it in thin slices and chew it well. The recipe given here is a very simple one but it can be varied by replacing half the wholemeal flour with other flours (e.g. buckwheat, cornmeal, rice, soya, millet or rye flour, etc.) or combinations of flours (see below). For a sweet bread add chopped nuts and dried fruit to the ingredients. To make a bread that will double as a meal, try adding leftover cooked vegetables or grains to the dough mix and then serve slices of the baked beans with a spicy sauce.

1½ lb (675g) wholemeal flour
2 teaspoons salt
Warm water (about ¾ pint
   (450ml))
A little vegetable oil

Makes 2 1 lb (450g) loaves

Combine the flour and salt in a mixing bowl and slowly stir in the warm water until you have a firm dough that comes away from the sides of the bowl. Knead the dough with vigour on a floured board for as long as you have the patience (at least 10 minutes). The more you knead the dough the better will be the texture of the finished bread. Form the dough into a ball, lightly oil your hands with vegetable oil and run them over the ball. Clean and dry the mixing bowl and place the dough in it. Cover it with a clean cloth and set it aside in a warm place for 24 to 36 hours. About every 8 hours, punch the dough down and turn it over. Divide the dough in half and place each half in a lightly oiled 1 lb (450g) bread tin. Cover and set aside in a warm place for another 3 to 5 hours. Preheat the oven to 300°F (150°C, gas mark 2). Place the bread in the oven and bake for 1½ hours or until the loaves slip easily out of the tins and sound hollow when tapped. Allow them to cool before using. Store unused bread wrapped in cling film in the refrigerator.

Variations
Replace the wholemeal flour by one of the following mixtures:

1 lb (450g) wholemeal flour
4 oz (100g) rye flour
4 oz (100g) cornmeal
OR
1 lb (450g) wholemeal flour
4 oz (100g) buckwheat flour
4 oz (100g) cornmeal

BAGELS

Bagels are at their best warm and fresh, straight from the oven, accompanied by hot coffee. For Jewish-style bagels see the variation below.

1 lb (450g) strong white flour
1 teaspoon salt
½ oz (15g) fresh yeast or 1 teaspoon dried yeast
¼ teaspoon sugar
4 fl oz (100ml) warm water
4 oz (100g) vegetable margarine, melted
2 tablespoons soya milk
Sesame seeds for topping

Makes about 20

Sift together the flour and salt. Dissolve the yeast and sugar in the water and set aside in a warm place until the mixture starts to bubble. Add the yeast mixture to the flour and salt and stir in the melted margarine. Mix well to form a firm but not stiff dough – you may need to add a little more water. Cover with a damp towel and set aside in a warm place for 1½ hours or until doubled in size. Preheat the oven to 375°F (190°C, gas mark 5). Pinch off small pieces of dough weighing about 2 oz (50g) and roll them into pencil-thick strips about 8 in (20cm) long. Form them into circles and brush them with the soya milk. Sprinkle with the sesame seeds. Transfer the bagels to ungreased baking trays. Leave for 10 minutes to rise and then bake in the preheated oven for 20 minutes or until nicely browned.

Variation

To make Jewish bagels put the unbaked bagels one by one into a large pan of boiling water and remove them as they rise to the surface. Transfer them to lightly greased baking trays and leave to rise for 10 minutes. Now brush the boiled bagels with soya milk, sprinkle them with sesame seeds and bake in a preheated oven at 400°F (200°C, gas mark 6) for 15 minutes or until nicely browned.

PAN BAGNAT

Pan bagnat is Provençal French for 'moist bread'. The recipe derives from the habit of dripping pieces of country bread into salad juices to mop them up. All types of bread may be used in this recipe, but smaller rolls, soft or crusty, are easier to manage. Prepare at least 1 hour before serving.

4 bread rolls
1 to 2 tomatoes, thinly sliced
4 to 5 black olives
4 to 5 stuffed olives
5 new potatoes, boiled, left to cool, and sliced
⅓ cucumber, sliced
½ small green pepper, cut into thin strips
½ small red pepper, cut into thin strips
1 small onion, cut into thin rings
1 bulb fennel, thinly sliced

Slice the top off each roll. Cover each roll with the tomatoes, olives, potatoes, cucumber, green and red pepper strips, onion and fennel. Season to taste with salt and black pepper. Drizzle the olive oil over the vegetables. Then sprinkle each with a few drops of vinegar. Put the top back on each roll. Leave for at least 1 hour so that the bread can absorb all the salad juices.

Salt and freshly ground black
    pepper to taste
4 tablespoons olive oil
Wine vinegar or cider vinegar

Serves 4

OLIVE BREAD

1 lb (450g) strong plain flour
½ teaspoon salt
4 tablespoons olive oil
1 oz (25g) fresh yeast, or 1
    tablespoon dried yeast
1 teaspoon sugar
7 fl oz (200ml) warm water
5 oz (150g) black olives,
    stoned and roughly chopped

Makes 4 small loaves

Put the flour and salt in a bowl with 3 tablespoons of the olive oil. Mix the yeast with the sugar and 4 tablespoons of the water. Leave to froth for about 15 minutes. Pour this mixture into the flour, and mix with the rest of the water. Work it to a stiff, sticky dough. Knead till the dough is smooth and elastic, about 10 minutes. Add the olives and continue kneading. Put the remaining tablespoon of oil into a clean bowl and turn the dough around in it until coated in oil, to prevent a dry crust forming. Cover with a damp cloth and leave to rise in a warm place for about 1½ hours until it doubles in size. Knead the dough again briefly and divide into 4 balls. Place them on an oiled baking sheet. Press each ball down gently. Let the dough rise once more, covered with the damp cloth for a further 1 hour. Preheat the oven to 475°F (240°C, gas mark 9). Brush the loaves with a little water. Bake for 30 minutes, or until they sound hollow when tapped on the bottom. This bread is best eaten the day it is made.

HERB BREAD

1½ lb (675g) wholemeal flour
2 tablespoons salt
½ oz (15g) fresh yeast
¾ pint (450ml) water
1 large onion, finely chopped
1 tablespoon each chopped
   fresh parsley, thyme, sage
   and mint
1 tablespoon olive oil
1 tablespoon celery seeds

Makes 1 large loaf

Mix the flour and salt together in a large bowl. Cream the yeast with a little of the water and leave until frothy. Add to the flour with the rest of the water, the chopped onion, the herbs and the olive oil. Mix to a smooth dough. Turn on to a floured surface and knead for 8 to 10 minutes to form a smooth, elastic dough. Put in a clean bowl, cover with a damp cloth and leave to rise in a warm place for about 1½ hours, or until doubled in size. Turn out again and knead for a further few minutes. Form into a round and place on an oiled baking sheet. Brush with water and sprinkle over the celery seeds. Cover and leave to rise in a warm place for a further 30 minutes, until almost doubled in size. Preheat the oven to 425°F (220°C, gas mark 7). Bake for 15 minutes, then lower the temperature to 375°F (190°C, gas mark 5) and bake for a further 20 to 25 minutes. The bread is cooked when it sounds hollow when tapped on its base.

HONEY AND OATMEAL BREAD

2 oz (50g) rolled oats
8 fl oz (225ml) boiling water
1 oz (25g) fresh yeast or 3
   teaspoons dried yeast
8 fl oz (225ml) lukewarm
   water
1 teaspoon sugar
4 oz (100g) honey

Place the oats in a mixing bowl and pour over the boiling water. Leave to stand for 20 minutes. Meanwhile dissolve the yeast in the lukewarm water and add the sugar. Set aside until the mixture starts to bubble. Add the honey, vegetable oil, salt and yeast

1 tablespoon vegetable oil
1 teaspoon salt
About 1½ lb (675g)
  wholemeal flour

Makes 3 1 lb (450g) loaves

mixture to the oats and mix well. Slowly beat enough flour into the mixture to make a firm but not stiff dough. Knead on a floured board for 5 to 10 minutes. Clean the mixing bowl, lightly grease the inside and put in the dough. Cover with a damp cloth and leave to rise in a warm place for 1 hour or until doubled in size. Preheat the oven to 400°F (200°C, gas mark 6) and grease 3 1 lb (450g) bread tins. Form the dough into 3 loaves and press into the tins. Cover with a damp cloth and leave to rise in a warm place for 45 minutes or until doubled in size. Bake the loaves for 5 minutes in the preheated oven then reduce the temperature to 350°F (180°C, gas mark 4) and bake for a further 40 to 45 minutes. To test if the bread is done, remove one loaf from a tin and tap the bottom; it should sound hollow when properly baked. If not, return the bread to the oven and leave a little longer. Remove from the oven, turn out of the tins and leave on wire racks to cool.

QUICK SPICED FLAT ONION BREAD

This white bread, which uses baking powder as a raising agent, has a quite distinctive taste.

1 lb (450g) self-raising flour
2 teaspoons baking powder
Pinch of salt
1 medium onion, finely
  chopped
1 teaspoon dried thyme
½ teaspoon ground cumin

Sift the self-raising flour, baking powder and salt into a bowl. Add the onion, thyme, cumin, coriander, cayenne pepper and oil and mix well. Make a hollow in a mixture and add the water slowly to form a smooth, soft dough that doesn't stick to the

½ teaspoon ground coriander
¼ teaspoon cayenne pepper,
  or more to taste
4 tablespoons olive oil
1 pint (550ml) water
Plain flour

Makes 8 flat rounds

sides of the bowl. Flour a working surface and knead the dough for 10 minutes or more. Divide the dough into 8 and roll each into a flat round about ¼ in (0.6cm) thick. Dust each with plain flour and cover with a clean, dry cloth. Leave for 30 minutes to rise. Preheat the oven to 475°F (240°C, gas mark 9). Place 2 lightly greased baking trays in the oven for 5 minutes after the oven has become hot. Put the bread on the trays and bake for 8 to 10 minutes or until the tops are lightly browned. Remove from the oven and allow to cool before serving.

WHOLEMEAL YEASTED PIZZA

This recipe is quite time-consuming if you have to make the dough especially for the pizza, therefore you may wish to use dough kept aside from the breadmaking session. Alternatively make double the amount of dough given in this recipe and make two pizzas, one for later use or to store in the deep freeze.

Dough
¼ oz (7g) fresh yeast
1 teaspoon brown sugar
¼ pint (150ml) lukewarm
  water
4 oz (100g) wholemeal flour
1 teaspoon salt
1 tablespoon vegetable oil

Sauce
2 tablespoons olive oil
1 lb (450g) ripe tomatoes,
  skinned and chopped (see
  page 30), or
14 oz (400g) tinned tomatoes,
  drained and chopped
2 tablespoons tomato purée

To make the dough
Cream the yeast and sugar together, add the warm water and set aside in a warm place for 15 to 20 minutes or until the mixture has frothed up. Combine the flour, salt and oil in a mixing bowl, add the yeast mixture and mix into a fairly soft dough which easily comes away from the sides of the bowl. Remove from the bowl and knead on a floured surface for 5 minutes to form a smooth, elastic dough. (Alternatively, place the flour, salt and oil into the bowl of a food processor and with the machine

1 teaspoon chopped fresh
   oregano, or ½ teaspoon
   dried oregano
Salt and freshly ground black
   pepper

Topping
1 medium onion, thinly sliced
2 oz (50g) mushrooms, wiped
   and sliced
1 medium green pepper,
   cored, seeded and thinly
   sliced
1 teaspoon chopped fresh
   oregano, or ½ teaspoon
   dried oregano

Serves 4

running, pour the yeast liquid through
the feed tube, process until the
mixture forms a ball around the knife
and then process for another 15 to 20
seconds to knead the dough.) Place the
dough in a clean bowl and cover with
a damp cloth; leave in a warm place
for 45 minutes to 1 hour until doubled
in size.

To make the sauce
Heat the oil in a saucepan, add the
tomatoes, tomato purée, oregano, salt
and pepper. Cook over a low heat,
stirring occasionally, for 15 minutes or
until all the excess liquid has
evaporated and you are left with a
thick purée. Cool. Preheat the oven to
475°F (240°C, gas mark 9).

To assemble the pizza
Punch down the dough with your fists
and knead lightly until smooth again.
Grease a pizza base, baking tray or
flan ring (about 12 in (30cm)
diameter). Roll the dough over the
base, keeping the centre ⅛ in (0.3cm)
thick while making the edges 1 in
(2.5cm) thick. Spread the sauce evenly
over the dough, but leave the edges
uncovered. Scatter the onion on top,
followed by the mushrooms and
pepper and finally sprinkle with the
oregano. Bake the pizza in the
preheated oven for 10 minutes, or until
the base is beginning to brown.

ARABIAN PITTA BREAD

Aish *(Egypt)*, khoubiz *(Gulf States)*, kesra *(Algeria)*, kmaj *(Lebanon)*, or pitta bread as we know it best in the West, are all varieties of the most common type of Arab bread. This is a slightly leavened, flat and usually round-shaped bread with a soft crust and a hollow or pocket running along the inside. The bread is cooked in a variety of ways but the basic principle is to provide a very hot oven or other baking utensil (e.g. a metal dome or sorj heated over an open fire until very hot, over which the bread dough is draped) in which the bread is cooked for a short period at a high temperature. This type of bread does not keep fresh for very long and should be eaten the day it is made. Arab bakers bake morning and evening. However, it does freeze successfully. To thaw, put the frozen bread straight into a very hot oven for 5 to 8 minutes, then serve immediately.

1 oz (25g) fresh yeast or ½ oz (15g) dried yeast
Pinch of sugar
About ¾ pint (450ml) warm water
1½ lb (675g) strong white flour
1 teaspoon salt
2 tablespoons oil (preferably olive oil)

Makes 8

In a small bowl mix the yeast, sugar and 4 tablespoons of the warm water into a smooth paste and set aside in a warm place for 10 to 15 minutes or until the mixture has frothed up. Put the flour and salt in a deep mixing bowl, make a well in the centre and pour in the yeast mixture, remaining water and oil. Knead the mixture into a smooth dough. If it is too hard add a little more water or, if too soft, a little more flour.

Turn the dough on to a lightly floured board and knead for about 15 minutes until smooth and elastic. Put the dough in a lightly oiled bowl, cover with a damp, clean cloth and leave in a warm place for 1½ to 2 hours until doubled in size.

Turn the dough on to a floured board, punch it down and divide into 8 equal portions. Roll these into balls and roll each ball out into an 8 to 10 in (20 to 25cm) round loaf. Leave them to rest on a floured surface, covered with a cloth, for 20 minutes.

Place a large baking sheet on the top shelf of a gas oven or the lowest shelf of an electric oven and preheat the oven to 475°F (240°C, gas mark 9). Now remove the baking sheet and carefully, grease the surface. Using 2 floured spatulas lift one of the loaves on to the baking sheet and then, if there's room, a second. Bake the bread in the oven for 5 minutes or until it puffs up and turns a delicate brown. Remove it from the oven and keep it warm in a cloth.

SFIHA (OPEN VEGETABLE PIE)

Pitta bread dough (follow previous recipe, using half of all the ingredients but all the yeast)
2 tablespoons vegetable or olive oil
1 large onion, finely diced
2 medium green peppers, seeded and finely chopped
2 medium red peppers, seeded and finely chopped
2 tablespoons finely chopped fresh parsley
Pinch of cinnamon and nutmeg
3 oz (75g) pine nuts, lightly toasted in the oven (chopped walnuts can be substituted)
Juice of 1 lemon
Salt and freshly ground black pepper to taste

Makes about 15

After the dough has risen for 1½ to 2 hours, roll out on a floured board until about ¼ in (0.6cm) thick. Cut into 6 in (15cm) circles and brush each circle with a little of the oil. Sauté the onion in 1 tablespoon of the oil until it is just softened, add the green and red peppers and continue cooking until they are just soft. Combine this mixture with the remaining oil and all the other ingredients and mix well. Preheat the oven to 400°F (200°C, gas mark 6). Place a heaped tablespoon of filling into the centre of each round and bring up the edges to form a lip around the mixture. As you make them, put them on to a greased baking sheet. Bake in the preheated oven for 20 to 25 minutes or until very lightly browned.

CHINESE PANCAKES

Serve these pancakes with savoury dishes. They make a pleasant change from rice or bread.

8 oz (225g) plain flour
¾ pint (450ml) boiling water
1 tablespoon sesame oil

Makes 14

Put the flour into a bowl, make a well in the centre and pour in the water. Mix to a dough, then knead on a floured board until smooth and elastic, at least 10 to 15 minutes. Divide into 14 portions. Roll each portion into a circle 4 in (10cm) in diameter. Paint each thinly with sesame oil. Place one round on top of another and roll out the 'sandwich' to make a pancake 6 in (15cm) in diameter. Make 6 more of these double pancakes. Heat a large frying pan on a low heat without oil and fry the double pancakes for about 1 minute per side, turning once so that each individual pancake is cooked on one side only. Keep shaking the pan to prevent the dough from sticking (do not use too high a heat). When cooked, separate each of the double pancakes to make 2 separate pancakes. Fold each single pancake into 4. Wrap in a warm cloth and keep warm until ready to serve.

BEANS

Beans is the term generally used to describe the seeds of plants in the legume family, which includes beans, peas and lentils. Cooked properly, they are a versatile, tasty, economical and nutritious food.

Beans contain two starches which are difficult to digest if they are not broken down before eating. For this reason it is essential that they are soaked and cooked for the correct time before consumption. This particularly applies to kidney beans, which also contain a harmful substance destroyed only by correct cooking. After soaking they should be boiled hard for 10 minutes, then the heat can be reduced to a simmer. This means that you need to remember to put the beans in to soak well in advance of the meal. The usual soaking time is twelve to twenty-four hours. Strictly speaking, lentils and split peas do not require soaking, but soaking does not do them any harm and speeds up the cooking time.

Weigh out the beans you require and cover them in cold water. Leave overnight, then drain, cover with fresh water and cook until tender, adding more water if the beans start to dry out.

Soaking and Cooking Times

Beans	Soaking times (hours)	Cooking times Without pressure (Hours)	With* (Minutes)
Aduki beans	2–3	1–1½	8–10
Black beans	8–12	1½–2	10–15
Black-eyed beans	8–12	1–1½	8–10
Broad beans	8–12	1½–2	10–15
Lima/butter beans	8–12	1½–2	10–15
Chickpeas	8–12	1½–2	10–15
Kidney beans, including Egyptian brown beans (ful medames)	8–12	1½–2	10–15
Great Northern beans	8–12	1½–2	10–15
Haricot beans	8–12	1½–2	10–15
Navy beans	8–12	1–1½	10–15
Pinto beans	8–12	1–1½	10–15
Red kidney beans	8–12	1–1½	10–15
Lentils	No soaking needed	20–30 minutes (small) 35–40 minutes (large)	6–10
Mung beans	8–12	45 minutes	10
Pigeon peas	8–12	1	10

Beans	Soaking times (hours)	Cooking times	
		Without pressure (Hours)	With* (Minutes)
Peas	8–12	1	10
Split peas	No soaking needed	20–30 minutes	6–10
Soya beans	24	3–4	30

* 15 lb pressure cooker.

Note Dried beans that you soak and cook yourself are the most nutritious and flavoursome sort to use but sometimes it's convenient to use canned cooked beans for an unexpected meal or to make a small amount of a particular dip or stuffing. In these instances the most easily available and perhaps the best canned beans are red beans and chickpeas. For this reason it is handy to have a couple of tins of each in the store cupboard.

Recipes for the soya bean product tofu are included in this chapter. Tofu, also called beancurd, is nowadays quite an easily available ingredient. It is a convenient and versatile food and a good source of protein, carbohydrate and minerals. Tofu, which is discussed in more detail in the Unusual Ingredients and Techniques chapter, is used in other recipes throughout the book. It is a particularly useful ingredient for making low-fat salad dressingss and, fluffed up with a little honey in a blender, it even makes a tasty dressing for fruit salads. Add tofu to soups, vegetables and salads to give extra body to them.

Amounts
1. 8 oz (225g) dried beans serves about 4 people.
2. Cover with 2 pints (1.1 litres) water per 8 oz (225g) beans
3. 1 volume dried beans gives 2 to 2½ volumes cooked beans.
4. 8 oz (225g) dried beans gives 1 to 1¼ lb (450-550g) cooked beans.

Cooking Tips
1. Thirty minutes before the end of the cooking period add 1 to 2 tablespoons cider vinegar to the pot. This reduces thet problem of intestinal gas.
2. Do not add salt to the beans until near the end of the cooking time, otherwise they harden and take longer to cook.
3. Other seasoning should be added later as well, since during cooking

beans seem to absorb and neutralize flavours. Lentils and split peas are the exception to this rule and can be seasoned at the start of cooking.

4. Chickpeas and red beans tend to foam when first cooked, remove the scum after 20 to 30 minutes and again later, if any more foams.
5. Cook twice as many beans as you need and store the extra in the fridge for 4 to 5 days. I find they keep best if only lightly covered. Use for making soups, salads, spreads, dips, mashed for rissoles, combined with cooked grains or as an accompaniment to a main meal.
6. Eat beans on their own; puréed in soups; in stews and casseroles; or cold in salads.
7. Slow cooking of beans develops their flavour. Fast cooking causes them to split and go mushy.

AUBERGINE AND RED BEAN STEW

A thick, red stew. Warm and satisfying.

1½ oz (40g) vegetable margarine
2 large onions, chopped
2 cloves garlic, crushed
1 large aubergine, diced
1 lb 14 oz (850g) tinned red kidney beans, drained
15 oz (425g) tinned tomatoes, drained (reserve liquid) and chopped
1 teaspoon dried basil
Salt and freshly ground black pepper to taste
2 tablespoons tomato purée
Vegetable stock made with 1 vegetable stock cube and 1 pint (550ml) water

Serves 4

Melt the margarine and sauté the onions and garlic until transparent. Add the aubergine and continue cooking for a further 5 minutes, stirring from time to time. Add the red kidney beans, the chopped tomatoes and their liquid, the basil and seasoning. Mix the tomato purée with the vegetable stock, pour in enough to cover the beans. Simmer, covered for about 30 minutes until everything is tender. Add extra vegetable stock if required. Serve piping hot in bowls.

SICILIAN BROAD BEANS

Quick to make if you use frozen vegetables. A winter dish with a taste of summer.

2 tablespoons olive oil
1 small onion, chopped
12 oz (350g) frozen broad beans
12 oz (350g) frozen garden peas
4 tablespoons vegetable stock or water
Pinch of grated nutmeg
Salt and freshly ground black pepper to taste
4 canned artichoke hearts
6 fresh mint leaves
½ teaspoon sugar (optional)
2 teaspoons wine vinegar (optional)

Serves 4

Heat the oil in a saucepan and fry the onion until transparent. Add the beans, peas, stock or water, nutmeg and seasoning. Cover the pan and simmer for 15 minutes. Drain the artichoke hearts and cut each into 6 pieces. Add to the other vegetables and continue to cook for a further 10 minutes. Chop some mint leaves, leave the others whole and stir them all into the pan. Leave to cool slightly before serving. If you wish to serve this dish cold, add the sugar and vinegar with the mint. Stir well, transfer to a serving dish and leave to cool. Chill for 15 minutes before serving.

FALAFEL OR TA'AMIA

Ta'amia and falafel are spicy, deep-fried bean croquettes. In Egypt ta'amia, made from dried white broad beans, are a national dish. The idea was imported to Israel where they substituted chickpeas and called the croquettes falafel. In both countries they are popular snack foods sold stuffed into split pitta bread, dressed with a hot sauce and accompanied by pickled vegetables. This recipe is for falafel, since chickpeas are easier to obtain than Egyptian white beans.

8 oz (225g) chickpeas, soaked overnight and drained
2 cloves garlic, crushed
2 medium onions, finely diced
1 bunch parsley, finely chopped
1 teaspoon ground coriander
1 teaspoon ground cumin
½ teaspoon turmeric

Cover the chickpeas in water and cook until soft (about 1 hour). Drain, and reserve the water for a soup, if you wish. Now mash the chick peas to a paste, which can be done by hand using a mincer or pestle and mortar, or in an electric blender. Combine the paste with the remaining ingredients

¼ teaspoon cayenne
½ teaspoon baking powder
Salt and freshly ground black
  pepper to taste
Vegetable oil for deep-frying

Serves 4 to 6

(except the oil) and mix together
thoroughly. Leave this mixture to rest
for 30 minutes and then form into 14
to 16 balls. If the balls are sticky, roll
them in a little flour. Deep-fry them in
hot oil until brown and crisp. Drain
on absorbent kitchen paper, and serve
hot (perhaps with one of the dips
given in the Starters chapter),
accompanied by a green salad and
pickles. Alternatively stuff the falafel
into split pitta bread, add salad and
pour over a dressing.

Variations

The baking powder can be replaced by the same weight of dried yeast.
If yeast is used, prove it with a little sugar and warm water before adding
it to the other ingredients, and leave the falafel mixture for 1 hour rather
than 30 minutes before cooking.

Cooked mashed vegetables, chopped nuts, caraway seeds or other
ingredients may be added to the basic mixture for more variety.

KIDNEY BEAN AND CIDER CASSEROLE

*A simple bean and vegetable dish given a very English flavour by the
use of cider in place of stock.*

2 tablespoons vegetable oil
2 cloves garlic, crushed
2 medium onions, sliced
1 medium green pepper,
  seeded and diced
2 medium courgettes, sliced
1 bay leaf
2 tablespoons tomato purée
8 oz (225g) cooked kidney
  beans
Salt and freshly ground black
  pepper to taste
8 fl oz (225ml) dry cider

Serves 4

Preheat the oven to 375°F (190°C, gas
mark 5).

Heat the oil in a heavy frying pan and
sauté the garlic and onions until
golden. Add the green pepper and
courgettes, stir and gently sauté until
softened. Pour the mixture into a
casserole dish and add the remaining
ingredients. Mix well, cover and bake
for 40 minutes.

CHINESE FRIED VEGETABLES AND MUNG BEANS

The variety of beansprouts we are most familiar with are cultivated from mung beans but the beans are good in their own right and also need less soaking and cooking than other beans.

8 oz (225g) mung beans
1 pint (550ml) water
2 tablespoons vegetable oil
1 clove garlic, crushed
1 medium onion, sliced
1 medium green pepper,
  seeded and diced
2 medium courgettes, sliced
4 oz (100g) mushrooms, sliced
2 teaspoons finely grated
  ginger root
1 tablespoon honey
2 tablespoons soya sauce
2 teaspoons cornflour

Serves 4

Soak the mung beans in the water for 2 to 4 hours and then simmer in the same water for 40 to 45 minutes or until tender. Drain and set the beans aside. Heat the vegetable oil in a heavy frying pan or wok and stir-fry the garlic, onion, green pepper and courgettes until softened. Add the mushrooms and ginger and stir-fry for a further minute. Blend together the honey, soya sauce and cornflour and pour the mixture over the vegetables. Add the mung beans and mix well. Stir and cook for a further 3 to 4 minutes then serve over hot boiled rice.

LENTIL-STUFFED APPLES

This dish is an unusual and nutritious combination of fruit, lentils and rice. It is convenient to prepare if you have leftover rice and lentils (or other combinations of pulses/grains). Serve it as the centre piece of a main meal accompanied by bulgar wheat and a green salad.

4 medium to large cooking
  apples, cored
4 fl oz (100ml) water
1 medium onion, diced
2 tablespoons vegetable oil
4 oz (100g) sultanas, soaked
  for 30 minutes and drained
4 oz (100g) lentils, cooked and
  drained
4 oz (100g) rice, cooked and
  drained

Preheat the oven to 300°F (150°C, gas mark 2).

Cut the tops off the apples and scoop out the flesh, leaving shells about ¼ in (0.6cm) thick. Mix the flesh with the water and cook, covered, until tender. Then remove the lid from the pan and simmer until the moisture has evaporated and the apple pulp is quite

½ teaspoon ground cumin
½ teaspoon turmeric
½ teaspoon salt
½ teaspoon freshly ground
  black pepper
1 teaspoon sugar

Serves 4

firm. Meanwhile sauté the onion in the oil until golden. Combine half the apple pulp, the onions, half the sultanas and all the remaining ingredients except the sugar. Mix well and stuff the apples with the mixture. Combine the remaining pulp and sultanas with the sugar and spread this mixture over the base of a lightly buttered baking dish. Pack in the stuffed apples and bake for 45 minutes.

NORTH AFRICAN BEAN POT

This unusual bean pot is very filling and nutritious. The recipe will make enough to feed 4 hungry people or 6 with a moderate appetite.

1 lb (450g) haricot beans,
  soaked overnight and
  drained
2 medium onions, 1 peeled
  and left whole, the other
  finely diced
4 cloves garlic, peeled
2 pints (1.1 litres) water
4 fl oz (100ml) vegetable oil
1 bunch parsley, finely
  chopped
1 teaspoon turmeric
1 teaspoon ground cumin
Salt and freshly ground black
  pepper to taste

Serves 4 to 6

Put the beans, the whole onion, whole cloves of garlic and water into a heavy pot and bring to the boil. Reduce the heat and simmer, covered, until the beans are tender – about 1 hour. Remove the onion and cloves of garlic (if you can find them) from the pot. Heat the oil in a heavy frying pan, add the diced onion and sauté until golden. Stir in the parsley, turmeric and cumin, mix well and pour the contents of the frying pan into the bean pot. Season to taste with salt and black pepper and simmer for 15 minutes. The beans should now be fairly dry. If they are not, scoop or drain off some of the liquid before serving and keep for later use in soups, etc.

FASOULIA

A haricot bean dish of Greek origin. Like the other bean dishes it can be served hot or cold depending on the weather, and whether it is being served as a starter, main or side dish. It is a very rich, garlicky dish and quite delicious. Serve with bread and salad.

8 oz (225g) haricot beans, soaked overnight and drained
4 fl oz (100ml) olive oil
1 small bulb of garlic cloves, peeled and crushed
1 bay leaf
1 teaspoon dried oregano
2 tablespoons tomato purée
Salt and freshly ground black pepper to taste
Juice of 1 lemon
½ small onion, diced

Serves 4

Put the beans, oil, garlic, bay leaf and oregano in a heavy pot and simmer over a low heat for 15 minutes. Remove from the heat and carefully pour in enough boiling water to cover the beans by about 1 in (2.5cm). Stir in the tomato purée and simmer the mixture, covered, over a very low heat for 2 to 2½ hours, until the beans are tender. Finally, season to taste with salt and black pepper, sprinkle in the lemon juice and serve garnished with the diced raw onion.

CHICKPEA AND VEGETABLE CURRY

A delicious, thick, spicy curry; serve it with rice, chapattis and chutney.

2 tablespoons vegetable oil
1 large onion, chopped
2 cloves garlic, crushed
2 teaspoons ground cardamom
1 teaspoon ground cumin
½ teaspoon chilli powder or hot pepper sauce
2 teaspoons ground turmeric
8 oz (225g) carrots, sliced
4 sticks celery, sliced
1 in (2.5cm) piece fresh ginger root, grated, or 1 teaspoon ground ginger
¼ pint (150ml) vegetable stock (see page 26) or water

Heat the oil in a saucepan, add the onion and garlic and cook until soft. Add the cardamom, cumin, chilli powder or hot pepper sauce and turmeric and cook, stirring continuously, for 5 minutes. Add the carrots and celery and mix well. Stir in the ginger, stock or water, and soya yogurt. Season to taste with salt and black pepper, bring to a very low simmer, cover and cook gently for 30 minutes. Add the mushrooms and chickpeas and continue cooking for 10 minutes. Sprinkle the coconut over the dish and serve.

¼ pint (150ml) soya yoghurt
Salt and freshly ground black
 pepper to taste
4 oz (100g) button
 mushrooms, rinsed
12 oz (350g) cooked
 chickpeas, drained (i.e.
 4 oz/100g dried chickpeas)
2 oz (50g) desiccated coconut,
 lightly dry-roasted until
 golden (see page 18)

Serves 6

RED BEAN ENCHILADAS

*Enchiladas are tortillas, the Mexican cornmeal pancakes, stuffed
with a bean and vegetable filling and baked with a sauce. Tortillas
are not difficult to make but obtaining the right ingredients for an
authentic flavour is not always easy, so do substitute 12 shop-bought
tortillas in this recipe if you wish.*

Tortillas
2 tablespoons vegetable
 margarine
12 fl oz (350ml) boiling water
4½ oz (125g) cornmeal
 (stoneground if possible)
5 oz (150g) wholemeal flour

Filling
2 tablespoons vegetable oil
1 onion, finely diced
1 green pepper, seeded and
 finely chopped
2 tablespoons finely chopped
 fresh parsley
1 lb (450g) cooked red kidney
 beans (i.e. about 8 oz/225g
 dried beans)
½ teaspoon ground cumin
½ teaspoon chilli powder
 (more or less may be used
 depending on how hot you
 like it)

To make the tortillas
Stir the margarine into the boiling
water in a mixing bowl and then stir
in the cornmeal. Set aside to cool to
room temperature and then mix in the
flour. Knead the dough for a few
minutes, adding more water if it is too
stiff and more flour if it is too soft.
Now divide the dough into 12
portions and roll each into a ball.
Flatten each ball on a lightly floured
board and roll it out to a circle about
6 in (15cm) in diameter. Flour the
rolling pin and board as necessary to
stop the dough sticking. Stack the
tortillas as you make them and cover
them with a cloth. Heat an 8 in
(20cm) ungreased nonstick frying pan
over a medium to high flame and cook
the tortillas one at a time for about 1

Salt to taste
1¼ pints (700ml) tomato
sauce (see page 30)

Serves 6

minute each side or until lightly
flecked brown on both sides. Stack
them and cover with a cloth to keep
them warm and pliable. If they are not
to be used immediately, they can be
softened before filling by heating them
for a few seconds on each side in a hot
frying pan.

To make the filling
Heat the oil in a saucepan and sauté
the onion for 2 minutes. Add the green
pepper and parsley and sauté for a
further 2 minutes. Add the cooked
kidney beans, cumin, chilli powder
and salt to taste. Add one-third of the
tomato sauce and bring to the boil.
Cover, reduce heat and simmer for 5
minutes. Remove from the heat.

To assemble the enchiladas
Preheat the oven to 350°F (180°C, gas
mark 4). Put 2 to 3 tablespoons of
filling on to each tortilla and roll them
up. Grease a baking dish and place in
it the filled tortillas seam-side down,
all in one layer if possible. Pour over
the remaining tomato sauce. Bake in
the preheated oven for 30 minutes or
until the sauce bubbles. Serve
immediately.

BURGUNDY BEAN CASSEROLE

*This is a rich and filling casserole, a good dish to serve for a dinner
with friends. It has a tempting aroma and the kitchen will be filled
with guests wanting to peer into the pot! Serve with crusty French
bread and a green salad.*

2 tablespoons vegetable oil
2 medium onions, chopped

Heat the oil in a large saucepan, add
the onions and cook over a moderate

2 cloves garlic, crushed
2 teaspoons cumin seeds
1 teaspoon dried oregano
1½ lb (675g) cooked red
    kidney beans (i.e. 12
    oz/350g dried beans)
1 lb (450g) potatoes, cut into
    large chunks
12 fl oz (350ml) red wine
¾ pint (450ml) water (or use
    the bean cooking water)
1 bay leaf
1 teaspoon dried thyme
14 oz (400g) tinned tomatoes
8 oz (225g) carrots, peeled
    and sliced
½ small to medium
    cauliflower, cut into florets
5 oz (150g) mushrooms, sliced
Salt and freshly ground black
    pepper to taste
Chopped fresh parsley to
    garnish

Serves 6 to 8

heat until softened. Add the garlic, cumin and oregano, stir and cook for 2 minutes. Add the cooked red beans, the potatoes, wine and water, bay leaf and thyme. Bring to the boil, reduce the heat, cover and simmer for 10 minutes. Add the tomatoes and carrots, stir well and simmer for a further 10 minutes. Add the cauliflower and simmer for a further 10 minutes. Add the mushrooms and season to taste with salt and black pepper. Simmer for a final 10 minutes then serve garnished with parsley.

FRIED TEMPEH

Fried tempeh is very nice served as a snack or side dish lightly sprinkled with salt or accompanied by a peanut sauce (see page 23).

Oil for deep-frying
12 oz (350g) tempeh, cut into
    sticks about 2 in × ¼ in ×
    ½ in (5cm × 0.6cm ×
    1.25cm)

Serves 4

Heat the oil (about 1 in /2.5cm) in a frying pan over a medium heat. Add half the tempeh sticks and fry, stirring, until they turn golden brown – about 5 minutes. Remove them with a small sieve or slotted spoon and set then to drain on absorbent kitchen paper. Repeat for the remaining tempeh. Combine the two batches of tempeh, sprinkle with salt and serve.

Variation: Seasoned and Fried Tempeh

2 cloves garlic, crushed
1 teaspoon salt
½ teaspoon freshly ground
  black pepper
1 teaspoon ground coriander
4 fl oz (100ml) water
Juice of 1 lemon or 3
  tablespoons tamarind water
12 oz (350g) tempeh, cut into
  sticks, as above
Oil for deep-frying

Mix the garlic, salt, black pepper, coriander, water and lemon juice or tamarind water together in a bowl and add half the tempeh sticks. Stir them about in the bowl to coat each stick with the seasoning. Leave to marinate for 5 to 10 minutes. Prepare a sieve over a bowl. Remove the sticks from the marinade and set them to drain for a few minutes in the sieve. Deep-fry the seasoned tempeh as directed in the recipe above.

STIR-FRIED BROCCOLI AND TOFU

Tofu or beancurd – the names are interchangeable – is very useful in stir-fry dishes. It absorbs the flavours of other ingredients and adds substance to vegetable meals. Pressed tofu (see page 22) is easier to stir-fry than the more fragile fresh tofu, but the best of all for stir-frying is the already deep-fried tofu. This may be bought in Chinese grocery shops. It is sold in slabs about 4 in (10cm) square and 1 in (2.5cm) thick and is recognizable by its slightly tough, yellow outer skin.

3 tablespoons vegetable oil
2 medium onions, coarsely
  chopped
3 cloves garlic, crushed
1 teaspoon grated fresh ginger
  root
2 large stalks broccoli –
  separate the florets from the
  stalks and chop; peel the
  stalks and cut diagonally
  into 1 in (2.5cm) lengths
12 oz (350g) drained, pressed
  tofu (or use deep-fried
  tofu), cut into chunks
¼ teaspoon hot pepper sauce
2 tablespoons natural soya
  sauce

Heat the oil in a wok or large frying pan and stir-fry the onions, garlic, ginger and broccoli stalks until the onions are just softened. Add the broccoli florets and stir-fry for 2 minutes. Add the tofu and hot pepper sauce, stir well and then cover the wok or pan and cook over a low heat for 2 to 4 minutes. The broccoli stalks should be just firm to the bite. At the last minute stir in the soya sauce and serve.

Serves 4

The vegan diet is often viewed as puritanical but, as I hope this book demonstrates, vegan food can be delicious as well as animal-product free. To escape from the stereotypical view of joyless vegan dishes I have chosen desserts that span the range from healthy to indulgent, but all of which taste wonderful.

ORIENTAL FRUIT SALAD

This fruit salad is made with an unusual mix of dried and fresh fruit. The addition of kirsch makes it really luxurious.

10 dried figs, cut into uneven pieces
10 fresh or dried dates, stoned and cut into quarters or pieces
2 oz (50g) whole, unskinned almonds
2 oz (50g) whole, unskinned hazelnuts
4 tablespoons kirsch
1 small honeydew or Ogen melon, peeled, sliced and cubed
14 oz (400g) tinned pineapple chunks in unsweetened juice

Serves 4

Mix the figs, dates and nuts together. Pour over the kirsch, cover and leave to marinate for several hours (or overnight, preferably). Mix the melon and pineapple chunks with the steeped fruit and nuts and pour over the juice from the pineapple. Put the salad into an attractive bowl and chill before serving.

FRESH PEACHES STUFFED WITH ALMONDS

4 large, firm peaches, halved and stoned
3 oz (75g) ground almonds
2 oz (50g) soft brown sugar
1½ oz (40g) soft vegetable margarine
½ teaspoon finely grated lemon rind

Serves 4

Preheat the oven to 350°F (180°C, gas mark 4). Scoop a little of the flesh from the centre of each peach half and put this into a bowl with the ground almonds, sugar, 1 oz (25g) of the margarine and the lemon rind. Beat until smooth with a spoon. Divide this stuffing between the peach halves, shaping it into neat little rounds. Dot each with the remaining margarine. Arrange the fruit in an oiled ovenproof dish and bake in the preheated oven for 20 to 30 minutes. Serve warm.

PEARS BAKED WITH CARDAMOM

A very good way of cooking pears that otherwise may not have a lot of taste. The spice gives them a delicate, subtle flavour.

4 large pears
2 tablespoons red wine
1½ oz (40g) soft brown sugar
1 teaspoon cardamom seeds

Serves 4

Preheat the oven to 350°F (180°C, gas mark 4). Peel, core and slice the pears. Put them in a shallow, ovenproof dish, sprinkle the sugar over them and add the wine. Sprinkle over the cracked cardamom seeds (crush them with a rolling pin). Bake in the preheated oven for about 25 minutes or until the pears are soft. Leave to cool, then serve.

FRUIT AND ALMOND IN HONEY SYRUP

Small individual pastries with a sweet fruit filling. They are rich and sweet and one or two with strong black coffee finishes off a meal delightfully.

1 lb (450g) dried fruit (figs, apricots, dates etc) very finely chopped
4 oz (100g) blanched almonds, chopped
4 oz (100g) fruit preserve or jam
1 teaspoon cinnamon
5 oz (150g) sugar
4 fl oz (100ml) water
3 tablespoons clear honey

To make the filling, combine the dried fruit, almonds, fruit preserve or jam, and cinnamon in a mixing bowl and knead them well together. Alternatively use a food processor to knead the mixture. Set the filling aside. Dissolve the sugar in the water in a heavy pan and bring to the boil. Reduce the heat and simmer for 10 minutes to form a syrup. Remove from

1 tablespoon rose water
8 oz (225g) filo pastry (12 sheets)
4 oz (100g) melted vegetable margarine

Makes 24

the heat and stir in the honey and rose water. Set the syrup aside.

Preheat the oven to 350°F (180°C, gas mark 4). Remove one sheet of filo pastry from the pack and brush it with melted margarine. Cut the sheet in half lengthwise and fold each half lengthwise again. You will end up with 2 sheets of pastry about 10 in × 6 in (25cm × 15cm). Divide the fruit mixture into 24 equal portions. Place a portion on the end of one of the pastry sheets and spread it across the bottom evenly. Fold the sides lengthwise over the filling and then roll it up like a carpet. Repeat with the remaining pastry and filling. Place the pastries on an oiled baking dish, seam side down, and bake in the preheated oven for 35 minutes. Remove from the oven and pour over the syrup then set aside to cool before serving. Store leftover pastries in a cool place in an airtight tin.

WINTER FRUIT MEDLEY

This is good as a dessert or a winter breakfast starter. It is especially tasty in late winter/early spring when the first unforced rhubarb is available.

2 oz (50g) dried prunes, stoned and chopped
2 oz (50g) dried apricots, chopped
1 oz (25g) sultanas
1 stick rhubarb, chopped
1 teaspoon lemon juice
1 cooking apple, cored and chopped

Put all the ingredients in a saucepan, except for the coconut. Cover with water and simmer for 20 minutes. Serve hot or cold, with honey to taste, topped with flakes of creamed coconut.

2 teaspoons honey, or to taste
Creamed coconut, flaked, to
  garnish

Serves 2

GRAPEFRUIT AND ORANGE BLUSH

A very simple but delicious dessert starter, or breakfast dish, served with a honey and mint sauce.

1 grapefruit
1 large orange
2 tablespoons clear honey
1 tablespoon apple juice
½ teaspoon chopped fresh
  mint
A few sprigs of fresh mint to
  garnish

Serves 4

Wipe the fruit, cut in half and remove any pips. With a curved knife or a saw-edged stainless steel knife, cut around the inside of the skin to loosen the flesh, remove the pith and cut the flesh into individual segments. Remove alternate grapefruit segments, replace with orange segments and vice versa with the orange. Serve either hot or well chilled. (To heat, place the filled orange or grapefruit halves under a moderate grill for 3 to 4 minutes.) Mix together the honey, apple juice and mint and serve in a side bowl with the fruit. Garnish with mint sprigs.

APRICOT FUDGE

Dried apricots are used in this recipe but you may substitute the same weight of other dried fruits.

2 oz (50g) dried apricots,
  finely chopped
3 oz (75g) plain chocolate,
  broken into pieces
12 oz (350g) sugar
4 fl oz (100ml) water
2 oz (50g) clear honey
4 oz (100g) vegetable
  margarine

Put all the ingredients into a heavy-based saucepan. Stir over a low heat until the margarine has melted, the sugar has dissolved and the mixture is homogeneous. Raise the heat a little and bring the mixture to the boil. If you have a kitchen thermometer boil the mixture to 240°F. If you do not

Makes 1 lb (450g)

have a thermometer, boil to the soft ball stage (drop a little of the boiling liquid into cold water; it will set but should remain soft when pressed). Now remove the pan from the heat and leave for 5 minutes. Meanwhile grease a 6 × 6 in (15 × 15cm) tin, or one of different dimensions but the same area. Beat the mixture with a wooden spoon until it starts to cool and then pour into the tin. Put the tin aside for the fudge to set. Cut into squares and serve. Store unused fudge in an airtight tin.

ROSE-FLAVOURED APPLES

This dessert is refreshing and cooling on a hot summer's day.

1 lb (450g) eating apples, cored
Juice of 1 lemon
2 oz (50g) caster sugar
2 tablespoons rose water
Cinnamon
Crushed ice

Serves 4

Grate the apples into a mixing bowl and stir in the lemon juice, sugar and rose water. Transfer to individual serving bowls, dust with a little cinnamon and top with crushed ice. Serve.

SUMMER PUDDING

There are only a few weeks in the year when all the soft fruit ingredients of this traditional British pudding are in season together but, during this time, it should definitely be on the menu. It's easy to make and looks and tastes splendid.

6 to 8 large slices white or brown bread, crusts removed
8 oz (225g) blackcurrants

Put a slice of bread on one side for the top. Use the remainder to line the base and sides of a 2 pint (1.1 litre) round dish. Make sure no gaps are left. Put

8 oz (225g) redcurrants
8 oz (225g) granulated sugar
6 tablespoons water
8 oz (225g) strawberries
8 oz (225g) raspberries

Serves 4 to 6

the blackcurrants and redcurrants into a saucepan and add the sugar and water. Bring to the boil and simmer for about 5 minutes or until barely tender, stirring all the time. Add the strawberries and raspberries and cook for 1 further minute. Turn the mixture carefully into the bread-lined dish. Place the extra slice of bread on top and bend over the tops of the bread from the sides towards the centre. Put a saucer on top, pressing down a little until the juice rises to the top. Put a weight on top of the saucer and leave overnight to set. Turn out on to a plate and serve.

CARROT ALMOND PUDDING

A fast, no-cook dessert (or breakfast dish).

2 tablespoons cornflakes
2 tablespoons soya milk
2 medium carrots, peeled and
   finely grated
3 tablespoons ground almonds
2 teaspoons lemon juice
2 teaspoons soft brown sugar

Serves 2

Soak the cornflakes in the soya milk then add the other ingredients. Mix well and leave to stand for 30 minutes, when the mixture should have become quite firm. Serve drizzled with honey or with puréed fruit such as apples or apricots.

TURKISH APPLE CAKE

This cake is delicious, and since it contains no fat it is a treat slimmers can enjoy.

1½ lb (675g) cooking apples,
   peeled, cored and chopped
Juice of 1 lemon
2 oz (50g) mixed nuts,

Preheat the oven to 350°F (180°C, gas mark 4).

Put the chopped apples into a large

chopped
2 oz (50g) sultanas
4 oz (100g) sugar
4 oz (100g) plain flour
Pinch of salt
1 teaspoon baking powder
½ teaspoon vanilla essence

Makes 2¼ lb (1kg) cake

bowl and sprinkle with the lemon juice. Combine the nuts, sultanas, sugar, flour, salt and baking powder and mix well. Stir this mixture into the apples. Stir in the vanilla essence and mix again. Pour the mixture into a lightly oiled cake tin and bake in the preheated oven for 20 minutes, or until lightly browned on top. Serve hot or cold. For a moister cake, add to the ingredients a little fruit juice or water.

Variation
This basic recipe can be adapted successfully for other fruits. Pears and plums together make a good combination.

FRUIT CHARLOTTE

An old favourite and a standby for using up stale bread.

12 oz (350g) fresh fruit
    (apples, plums, cherries etc)
3 oz (75g) vegetable margarine
6 slices wholemeal bread
3 oz (75g) soft brown sugar
Juice and rind of 1 lemon or 1
    orange

Serves 4

Preheat the oven to 350°F (180°C, gas mark 4).

Wash, peel and cut up the fruit (stone cherries or plums). Melt the margarine and dip the bread into it until it is well covered. Line a pie dish with 4 slices of the bread, cut to shape, and fill it up with the fruit, the sugar, and the juice and rind of the lemon or orange. Cover with the remaining 2 slices of bread and bake in the preheated oven for about 45 minutes until the fruit is tender and the bread crisp. Sprinkle a little sugar over the charlotte and serve hot.

PLUM STRUDEL

3 oz (75g) vegetable margarine
3 oz (75g) strudel (filo) pastry
4 oz (100g) fresh breadcrumbs
6 oz (175g) sugar
1 teaspoon ground cinnamon
2 lb (900g) plums, washed, stoned and roughly chopped
Icing sugar

Serves 4 to 6

Preheat the oven to 400°F (200°C, gas mark 6).

Melt the margarine. Spread one sheet of strudel (filo) pastry on a large flat surface and brush with the melted fat. Place another pastry sheet on top, and brush again. Repeat until all the pastry is used up. Mix the breadcrumbs, sugar and cinnamon together. Spread the prepared plums evenly on top of the pastry. Sprinkle the crumbs and sugar mixture over this. Keep the edges of the pastry clear. Fold over 2 in (5cm) all round the pastry, then fold the long edges over to form a roll. Place the roll, seam side down, on a baking sheet and bend into a horseshoe shape. Brush with any remaining melted margarine. Bake in the preheated oven for 40 minutes, until golden and crisp. Sprinkle with icing sugar and serve.

STICKY RICE WITH MANGOES

This Thai dessert is everyone's favourite during the mango season of that country. If glutinous rice is unavailable, short grain pudding rice may be substituted.

½ pint (275ml) medium coconut milk
2 oz (50g) white sugar
½ teaspoon salt
10 oz (275g) glutinous (sticky) rice, soaked overnight, drained, cooked and kept warm
4 ripe mangoes, peeled,

In a large mixing bowl stir together 8 fl oz (225ml) of the coconut milk with the sugar and salt and stir until the sugar dissolves. Stir in the still warm cooked rice, cover and set aside for 20 or 30 minutes. Meanwhile, simmer the remaining coconut milk in a small pan, uncovered, for 10 minutes. Place

halved, stones removed, and sliced crosswise

Serves 4 to 6

the sticky rice in the centre of a serving plate, arrange the mango slices around it, sprinkle the rice with the simmered coconut milk and serve.

LUCKY BAG ORANGES

In this recipe oranges are stuffed with melon, hazelnuts and tofu mixed with a little ground ginger. It is an unusual mixture of ingredients but their individual flavours do combine well in this visually pleasing dish.

4 large oranges
½ just ripe small honeydew
   melon, deseeded
1 oz (25g) hazelnuts, chopped
1 to 2 tablespoons clear honey
4 oz (100g) tofu
¼ to ½ teaspoon ground
   ginger

Serves 4

Wipe the oranges and cut off the top third of each one. With a sharp stainless steel knife or a grapefruit knife, carefully cut out all the orange flesh keeping the segments as whole as possible and removing any white pith. Reserve the empty orange skins. Squeeze the juice from the sliced-off tops into a bowl and toss with the orange segments. Scoop out the flesh from the melon with a teaspoon or melon baller and mix with the oranges. Add the nuts and honey. Leave to chill, covered, for 30 minutes. Cream the tofu and ginger together. Fill the empty orange skins with the prepared fruit and top with small spoonfuls of the tofu mixture.

PEARS IN VERMOUTH AND VANILLA

Pears were believed by the Celts to be aphrodisiacs. With vermouth in the recipe too this dessert could provide a passionate end to a meal. Perhaps it should be reserved for special occasions.

4 only just ripe pears
   (Williams pears are

Put the pears in a shallow pan with the lemon juice, vanilla pod or essence

recommended), cored,
peeled and quartered
Juice of 1 lemon
2 in (5cm) piece of vanilla
pod, or 1 teaspoon vanilla
essence
6 fl oz (175ml) dry vermouth
1 oz (25g) granulated sugar

Serves 4

and vermouth. Simmer gently for 12 to 15 minutes. Lift the pears out with a slotted spoon and arrange them on a serving dish. Add the sugar to the juices remaining in the pan and boil for 3 minutes or until thickened. Strain the juices over the pears, cool and then chill before serving.

BAKED GINGER AND CITRUS BANANAS

This Southeast Asian dessert is particularly good and lends itself well to Western tastes and the Western kitchen.

2 oz (50g) soft vegetable
margarine
2 oz (50g) white sugar
1 tablespoon lemon juice
1 tablespoon orange juice
½ teaspoon cinnamon
1 teaspoon grated lemon rind
2 teaspoons finely chopped
ginger root
6 bananas, peeled, cut in half
crosswise

Serves 6

Preheat the oven to 375°F (190°C, gas mark 5).

Beat together the margarine and sugar and then beat in the lemon and orange juice, cinnamon, lemon rind and ginger root. Lightly grease a shallow baking dish and arrange the banana pieces on the bottom. Pour over the butter/ginger mixture and bake in the preheated oven for 15 minutes. Serve immediately.

BLACKBERRY AND APPLE CRUMBLE

This is a simple but very enjoyable dessert. It looks appetizing and the chopped nuts in the crumble give it an interesting texture. If you wish, use more blackberries and fewer apples. The same recipe can be followed to make pear, apricot or other stewed fruit crumble.

4 large, firm dessert apples
8 oz (225g) blackberries
2 tablespoons clear honey
8 oz (225g) wholemeal flour
5 oz (150g) vegetable

Preheat the oven to 350°F (180°C, gas mark 4).

Peel, core and thickly slice the apples. Put the apples, blackberries and honey

margarine
4 oz (100g) dark brown sugar
3 oz (75g) hazelnuts, coarsely
  chopped

Serves 4

in a pan, bring to a gentle boil, reduce heat, cover and simmer for 5 minutes or until the apples are just tender. Stir occasionally. Transfer the mixture to a shallow baking dish and pour over any honey syrup left in the pan. Rub the flour and margarine together in a mixing bowl to form a crumble with the texture of coarse breadcrumbs (alternatively use a food processor). Stir in the sugar and hazelnuts and spread the crumble evenly over the top of the fruit. Bake in the preheated oven for 45 minutes or until nicely browned. Serve hot or cold.

UNCOOKED DATE AND NUT SWEETS

These date and nut sweets are very good with coffee at the end of a meal. They are sweet and quite filling, and two or three at a time are usually enough. Unused sweets keep very well for two to three weeks in an airtight tin.

8 oz (225g) almonds, dry-
  roasted (see page 18)
8 oz (225g) dates, finely
  chopped
Icing sugar

Makes about 20

The almonds need to be coarsely ground and this can be accomplished by putting them into an electric grinder or blender and then pulsing the machine for 2 to 3 seconds. Alternatively, crush the almonds by placing them under a very dry clean cloth and rolling them with a rolling pin. Combine the dates and almonds in a small bowl and work them together with your fingers to form a homogeneous mixture. If your fingers get too sticky dust them with a little icing sugar. Form the mixture into a ball. Dust a work surface and rolling pin with icing sugar and roll out the date and almond ball to form a slab about ½ in (1.25cm) thick. Cut this into 1in (2.5cm) squares and dust them with icing sugar. Arrange the sweets on a plain white plate and serve.

Variation
Before dusting with icing sugar, sprinkle the sweets with desiccated coconut.

PEACHES WITH FRESH STRAWBERRY SAUCE

A dessert to be made during those summer months when peaches and strawberries are in season and a punnet of strawberries, almost overripe, can be bought cheaply at the end of the day.

4 large ripe peaches
8 oz (225g) very ripe
　　strawberries
Juice of 1 orange
3 tablespoons Armagnac (or
　　another brandy)

Serves 4

Skin the peaches by making a small nick in the skin at the stalk end and plunging them into a bowl of boiling water for 45 seconds; the skin should slip off easily. Place each peach in a small glass bowl. Wash, hull and drain the strawberries (reserve 4 firm ones) and place in a liquidizer with the orange juice and brandy. Blend until smooth and fairly thick. This gives a textured sauce and you may prefer to sieve it. Spoon the sauce evenly over the peaches. Chill for 1 hour. Garnish with the reserved strawberries, sliced, before serving.

BLUSH PINK GRANITA WITH RASPBERRY SAUCE

Use a Californian 'Blush' or a Portuguese rosé wine for this granita (a light-textured water ice). Eat soon after making before granitas are inclined to set solidly if stored for any length of time.

6 oz (175g) caster sugar
2 fl oz (50ml) water
Finely grated rind and juice of
  1 large orange
Finely grated rind and juice of
  ½ lemon
1 bottle (750ml) Blush or rosé
  wine

Serves 4 to 6

Put the sugar and water into a saucepan and add the citrus rind and juice. Bring to the boil, stirring to dissolve the sugar. Simmer for 3 or 4 minutes. Allow to cool, then add the wine and strain into a glass or stainless steel freezer tray. Put in the coldest part of the freezer or fridge icebox. After 1 hour, the syrup will begin to freeze. Stir the half-frozen ice crystals well with a metal spoon. Return to the freezer and stir every 30 minutes until the crystals form an even mass and the granita holds together. Store in the icebox or least cold part of the freezer until ready to serve. Serve the granita scooped on to individual glass plates, surrounded by a pool of raspberry sauce (recipe below), or in glasses with the sauce poured over.

RASPBERRY SAUCE

Raspberry sauce is also wonderful poured over fresh peaches, figs and mangoes.

12 oz (350g) raspberries, fresh
  or frozen
3 tablespoons granulated
  sugar

Put the raspberries and sugar into an enamel saucepan, cover and simmer over a low heat until the juices run. Allow the fruit to cool, then rub it through a fine nylon sieve. Chill before serving.

SHERBET

Sherbets are sweet fruit syrups, originally from Persia, served very cold on their own for sipping or as a drink with iced water or soda water (fizzy sherbet). They can also be used for making soya milk shakes. Almost any fresh fruits may be used but cherries, strawberries, raspberries, blackberries, apricots and grapes are particularly suitable.

Use 1 lb (450g) fruit to make enough syrup for a dozen or more drinks. Put the fruit (stoned if necessary) and an equal weight of sugar in a large bowl. Mash the fruit slightly and mix well. Cover and leave overnight, or for 6 to 8 hours at least. Strain the mixture through a muslin bag or fine sieve until all the syrupy liquid has been drained off. Bottle the syrup and store in the refrigerator. Serve 1 or 2 tablespoons in a glass of iced water.

If apples are used they must be peeled and grated first. Also add a squeeze of lemon juice to the mixture to prevent discolouration.

WATER ICES

Sorbets were originally a Turkish iced drink similar to a sherbet but nowadays the word is used to describe water ices. These are made from sugar, water and a flavouring such as fruit juice. Successful water ices require a precise amount of sugar. They also need lots of stirring and a quick freezing process to prevent crystallization of the water into icy lumps. The problem of crystallization is avoided if you have an ice-cream machine but, if not, it is easier to make a clear, less sweet water ice with, say, a coffee, fragrant tea or lemon juice flavouring. In ices such as these the taste is less affected by the presence of large water crystals. It is important that in any water ice you make you use mineral or filtered water that is free of chlorine.

Below is a general method for making water ices followed by a more specific recipe.

General Method for Making Water Ices

If your refrigerator freezer box is small then use the ice trays for freezing the water ice. If you have a large ice box or a deep freeze then use a more conveniently sized freezer-proof plastic container. About an hour before mixing the frozen dessert, reduce the temperature in the refrigerator to its coldest setting. Now combine the water ice ingredients, put the mixture into the ice trays or plastic container and then freeze. Stir it at intervals of about 15 minutes until the mixture is half frozen. Now leave it to freeze hard. Alternatively, allow it to semi-freeze then turn the mixture into a bowl and beat thoroughly with an electric whisk (or liquidizer). Return the mixture to the container and refreeze until hard (between 1 and 4 hours depending on the mixture).

Note Stirring or whisking the water ice during the first half of the freezing process helps to counteract the formation of ice crystals and flakes.

ORANGE AND LEMON WATER ICE

Finely pared rind and juice of
  2 medium lemons
Finely pared rind and juice of
  1 medium orange
4 oz (100g) caster sugar
1 pint (550ml) water

Serves 4 to 6

Put the lemon and orange rind in a pan, add the sugar and water and bring to the boil. Gently boil for 10 minutes and set aside to cool. Stir in the lemon and orange juice and strain the mixture into the container for freezing. Now follow the general method given above.

Weights and Measures

Weights		Liquids	
Imperial	Approximate metric equivalent	Imperial	Approximate metric equivalent
½ oz	15g	¼ teaspoon	1.25ml
1 oz	25g	½ teaspoon	2.5ml
2 oz	50g	1 teaspoon	5ml
3 oz	75g	2 teaspoons	10ml
4 oz	100g	1 tablespoon	15ml
5 oz	150g	2 tablespoons	30ml
6 oz	175g	3 tablespoons	45ml
7 oz	200g	1 fl oz	25ml
8 oz	225g	2 fl oz	50ml
9 oz	250g	3 fl oz	75ml
10 oz	275g	4 fl oz	100ml
11 oz	300g	5 fl oz (¼ pint)	150ml
12 oz	350g	6 fl oz	175ml
13 oz	375g	7 fl oz	200ml
14 oz	400g	8 fl oz	225ml
15 oz	425g	9 fl oz	250ml
1 lb	450g	10 fl oz (½ pint)	275ml
2 lb	900g	15 fl oz (¾ pint)	450ml
3 lb	1.4kg	20 fl oz (1 pint)	550ml
		1¾ pints	1 litre
		2 pints	1.1 litres

Exact conversion: 1 oz = 28.35g

Oven Temperatures

°F	°C	Gas mark
225	110	¼
250	130	½
275	140	1
300	150	2
325	170	3
350	180	4
375	190	5
400	200	6

°F	°C	Gas mark
425	220	7
450	230	8
475	240	9

British and American Equivalents

This book was written for a British readership. To help the American cook with the system of measurement used, here is a conversion table showing imperial weights with their American cup equivalent.

British	American	British	American
8 fl oz	1 cup	4 oz white flour	1 cup
½ pint/10 fl oz	1¼ cups	4 oz green beans, chopped	1 cup
16 fl oz	1 pint	7 oz dried lentils	1 cup
1 pint/20 fl oz	2½ cups	7 oz cooked lentils	1 cup
2 pints/40 fl oz	5 cups	3½ oz mangetout	1 cup
2 tablespoons	⅛ cup/½ tablespoons	9 oz miso (Japanese soya-bean paste)	1 cup
8 tablespoons	½ cup	2 oz broken noodles	1 cup
4 oz ground almonds	1 cup	6 oz diced onion	1 cup
5 oz almonds, unblanched	1 cup	2 oz parsley, finely chopped	1 cup
4½ oz dried apricots	1 cup	6 oz peanut butter	1 cup
7 oz aubergines, diced	1 cup	5 oz peanuts	1 cup
6 oz bamboo shoots, drained and sliced	1 cup	3½ oz black peppercorns	1 cup
4 oz beancurd, drained	1 cup	6 oz canned pineapple chunks, drained	1 cup
6 oz beans (canned)	1 cup	6 oz raisins or sultanas	1 cup
3 oz beansprouts	1 cup	8 oz dry rice (brown or white)	1¼ cups
3½ oz broccoli (fresh), sliced	1 cup	6 oz sesame seeds	1 cup
4 oz bulgar wheat	1 cup	8 oz cooked spinach	1¼ cups
4 oz cabbage, shredded, firmly packed	1 cup	1 lb raw spinach	5 cups
4 oz cauliflower, in florets	1 cup	6½ oz cooked red beans	1 cup
4 oz cooked chickpeas	1 cup	8 oz granulated sugar	1 cup
2 oz flaked, unsweetened		6 oz brown sugar	1 cup
		9 oz canned tomatoes	1 cup

coconut	1 cup	8 oz tomatoes	2 medium tomatoes
3½ oz coriander seeds	1 cup	9 oz tomato paste	1 cup
4 oz sweetcorn kernels	1 cup	7 oz vegetable fat	1 cup
6 oz cornflour	1 cup	4 oz walnuts, chopped	1 cup
5 oz courgettes, sliced	1 cup	6½ oz water chestnuts, drained	1 cup
3½ oz cumin seeds	1 cup	1 oz yeast	1 cup
8 oz cooking dates	1 cup		
4½ oz wholewheat flour	1 cup		

INDEX